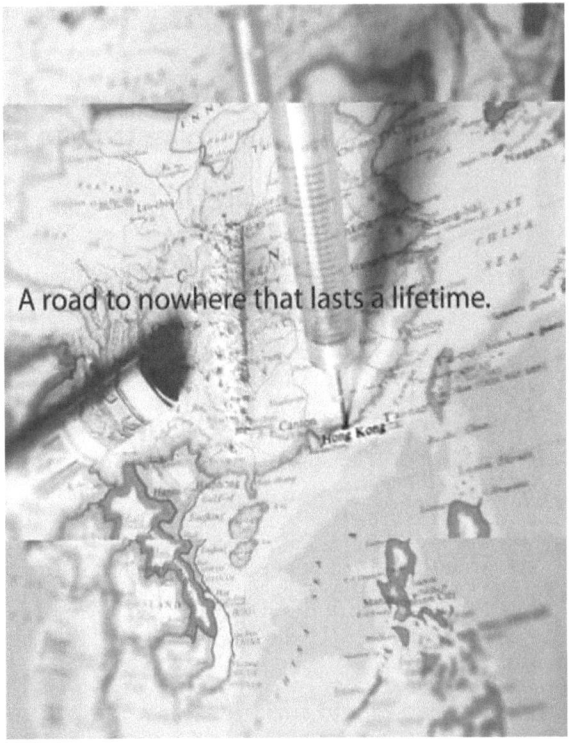

If the drugs don't kill you the death sentence will!
Edward Cole

When you're just nineteen and doing time in Hong Kong, you realise that dreams can turn into disaster.
I Universe

Cross over into an underworld you'll be glad you're only reading about.
Allan Kempton

There is no intermission with drugs. Cocaine and heroin continuously search for new victims.
Lynn Blair

An amazing read, it has hit my brain again and again like cocaine!
Charles Muller

Sun, sand, sea and surf, the balmy climate and prospect of new things, that was the dream before the disaster.
Mark Penn

For Sharm there was Red. Then there was cocaine which also seemed completely harmless.
Diadem books

Addiction does not make exception for good intentions! Adulthood and its shackles could come later.
L Browning

Brilliant and different an education every teenager should have!
Jane Knight

A powerful projection of naivety and teenage innocence!
Silk FM

The author writes from the perspective of someone who herself has survived the odds.
Carmen Elizabeth

Formatting by Dave Wassink

Scraping the Sky

All Rights Reserved.
Copyright © 2008 2014 Mary Jane Pearce

No part of this book may be reproduced or transmitted in any form or by any means, graphic, electronic, or mechanical including photocopying, recording, taping or by any information storage or retrieval system without permission in writing from the publisher. Not to be otherwise circulated in any form of binding or cover other than which it is published and without a similar condition including this condition being imposed on the subsequent purchaser. All characters in this publication are fictitious and any resemblance to real persons, living or dead is purely coincidental.

Published by Bonker Books
www.bonkerbooks.com
Printed in the United Kingdom

ISBN 978-0-9558184-3-1
A catalogue record for this book is available from the
British Library
For the Preservation of World Wildlife

This book should be included in the education curriculum, from the age of 14 and upwards. Youths would get so much more out of reading this than they would the likes of The Merchant of Venice or Macbeth. We live in the 21st century and yet books like this are still not included. Well detailed, it tells a powerful story of teen travel and naivety along the often trod back packing trail through Asia. The characters spring to life as do the events as to how the book begins. This is a dangerous story of a teenage girl who puts her trust in others who clearly only have their own interests at heart. It leads you through a life many of us find hard to comprehend. If you have young teenagers it could save their lives.
Nick Alexander
Silk FM radio

For life because there's so much more to it.

Scraping the Sky

And so we begin to run
Our very first joint
The intention was fun
Next a bottle of rum
A touch of snow
And the brain goes numb
And so the depression does come
You shiver shake and want to scream
Only one thing left the brown smoke screen
To combat your life and kill all your dreams
The dragon is restless aloud it so screams
Fully loaded with busted seams
Only those on the wagon will hear you scream

Little Apple

Tai Tam Gap is a young offenders' prison set high in the mountains of Hong Kong. I was nineteen, cold and confused. A third of the prison was made up of Thais, Filipinas, and Cambodians. The rest was inhabited by local Hong Kong girls, and girls from Mainland China. Just like the bullies back home the screws got under your skin, learned your weaknesses and pushed your fear buttons whenever they had a spare moment. The worst intimidator was officer Gum, a twenty-stone bully who often appeared and sought out the shy. One morning she randomly picked on a Thai girl, at first she just spat abuse and nasty comments but reducing the girl to tears alone wasn't enough. She took one of the bras from a locker, tied it around the girl's head and tightened it. Pulling and pushing with venom, she forced her blindfolded victim to the floor. Only when broken and begging, hands held high while accepting a dig in the ribs, did Officer Gum back off and leave. The other monster was Mush Tang, "who merely ran laundry," not the army barracks he thought he did. Being the only guy in the place did nothing except corrupt his crummy little mind even more than it already was. He often came to the dorm bars before and after work. From there, he would eye us up, shout sick comments, blow smoke in our faces, and tease the Cambodians, who always swallowed his abuse in silence. Winter was good because he hated the wet meaning that we saw less of him. One morning, I sensed a storm coming and was surprised to see him appear at all. Pacing the ground he lit up and pulled hard on a cigarette, passing smarmy comment on those closest to the bars, he followed it up with a barrage of Chinese abuse. He was sparking up his second fag when the storm broke. Stamping it out, he shoved his dick to the side of his trousers tightened his collar and hurried towards the main building. I got up from my table and moved towards the gated entrance. Though cold, I held the bars and leant my head between them. An electrical current in the sky and thunder followed, a few seconds later and blobs of Asian rain fell in its bucket loads, hitting the ground like tiny bombs, churning into murky waters reminding me of the spoon and syringe I'd once owned. Looking at the colours for long periods of time kind of mesmerized me, making it easier to pretend I didn't exist, that the world was a better place, and that humiliation, hurt and betrayal didn't exist. My thoughts washed away, I knew it was just wishful thinking. Feet rooted to the ground, I felt sheets of wind pass over my already ice cold skin. Withdrawal my worst enemy, I was now fighting the depression that follows it.

During the day boredom became biggest problem. Apart from polishing my teeth and boots nothing much else happened. Evening was better, as it always led to another day and brought out the glow bugs. It was the coolness of the mountains that attracted them, the air was thinner and cleaner than downtown. They reminded me of bright bees singing softly as they embraced the night with flashing lights before shooting off elsewhere leaving a trail of stardust behind them. Unlike most people, they knew where they were going, what they were searching for, and where to find it. They were a constant reminder of freedom and of how fast we can fall through innocence, ignorance and the influence of others. As sheets of torrential rain fell I shivered, pushing my head further through the bars I watched it cleanse the ground. As the water ran over my cheeks, I was reminded of the blood that had once run there. My first boyfriend had been a bully, and the scar would always be with me. I had thought Asia would be different, better, a place to explore, a place to find myself. Instead, I'd got lost, found an easy way to find confidence and mask everything I didn't like about life. My thoughts turned to my dad. I could hear him in my head. It was always the same, always about money! Always stressed he found it easier to shun and shout rather than show love. Our house had been less than basic, like our clothes, most of the contents were hand-me-downs. This I could live with, just not the judgement and spite of others. As I had got older dad seemed to get worse. While he spent what he earned on other women, my mother went without and we became easy pickings at school in our shoddy seconds. We were often taken to the verbal cleaners because of our appearance, and it wasn't nice. Like money, time was something my dad didn't have, and time was what we needed. Like my thoughts, the rain didn't let up. Somewhere out there, the bastard responsible for all this was sunning it up. This, I found hard to swallow. Not even the cold showers, inmate or screw hostility, came close. I had seen many foreign inmates humiliated until the pain caused them to snap, giving them a free ticket to the holding cells below. Fortunately for me, I had not been on the receiving end of any bored officer's abuse. Whether it was my British citizenship, or the fact that I dedicated so much time to studying their language, I didn't know, only that I was grateful to survive each and every monotonous day and those bloody boots, they made us shine.

As the rain subsided, it all came back like yesterday…

Wheels bumping along the baked runway, my plane arrived around seven. I could feel the energy of the city long before embracing it. Outside the heat was stifling, causing lameness in both my lungs and limbs. As I headed towards the terminal the heat showed no signs of letting up. The airport was full of activity and outside there was no shortage of cabs. As I stepped into one, I asked the driver to find me some cheap digs. The city roads were like conveyor belts that snaked across, under and over each other. Strobes strained my eyes and skyscrapers seemed to dance high into the rhythm of the night, from where they shone down upon the city revealing its luminous beauty. Eventually we turned off the highway and headed down some of the less-congested streets until my driver stopped outside a café. Above it hung the name 'Min'. It should have said 'Ming's' but the last two letters had slipped and hung dangerously above the entrance.

"It's okay?" The cabbie cocked his head to one side before pointing upwards. At first I didn't answer. The building was as dilapidated as the next one, so choice wasn't really an issue. Too exhausted to care, I paid him in crisp new dollars and stepped onto the hectic pavement. Rushing along the busy streets, Cantonese folk slowed for one thing only! I could see and smell 'fast food' from every angle. Despite the fact that they consumed vast amounts of it, the Chinese were a nation of stick insects who made me feel rather plump in comparison. The heat had killed my appetite, but thirsty I was. Below the bedsit was a café. Stepping inside the smell was horrid, just how I imagined overcooked and outdated food to be. I watched five guys shoving one another playfully while a new hand of cards was dealt. Tearing my eyes away from the fast card flicks I asked the waiter for a bottle of water.

"OK, give me five!" Busy, he bustled about the place like a blue bottle.

An Indian boy to my right sat tapping his table. Eyes wide, he was elsewhere. Out back I could hear crockery being slammed about. Outraged by the noise, the waiter shouted a few obscenities towards the kitchen opening. Back to the five lads playing poker and the tension was growing. As the stakes increased so did their anxieties. A few moments later and the whole game went pear-shaped. One of the taller lads rose, cleared the table of cash, knocked the waiter flying, pushed me hard against the door and did a runner. As the others tore after him the contents of the table crashed to the ground. The waiter stopped dead in his tracks, shouted after them and grabbed a mop. Laughing behind his menu, the Indian lad had sunk down into his seat. Passing on the water I made my way into the bedsit entrance next door.

The lobby was poorly lit, and the carpet had seen better days. I pushed the lift button, but nothing happened. Hearing someone on the stairs I turned.

"Nothing much works ere, especially that," an Australian voice said. "I'm Puk, you?"

"Sharm...!" I squinted, trying to get a better view of him.

The voice and silhouette became clearer as he reached the last few stairs. Leaping them, the tall lean figure landed a few feet from me.

"I'll catch you soon then."

With that he left the building.

Upstairs, almost drowning in a high backed chair, a well-preserved woman sat bolt upright behind a desk. She took a long cigarette from her mouth.

"I'm Anna," she was firm, but friendly, "you want a room?"

"Depends how much?"

"Have passport?"' She stubbed her fag out and moved

round to the front of her desk, hand out-stretched she examined my luggage.

I unzipped my bag and handed it to her. Without wasting any further time she pulled out a box of documents, added my passport without checking it, and slammed it shut.

"Pay ten dollar by day, okay?" Expectant her eyes were wide. A key suddenly dangled from her hand, exchanging it for the cash I then followed her instructions to the end of the corridor and opened my door. The room contained an oval bed with a patchwork cover. The ceiling was made up of paint blisters that had popped from age and the overall smell was stale. The fallen paint flecks made the dragon on the rug look like it had chickenpox. Jet lagged, I fell on the bed and closed my eyes. I woke some hours later to the sound of snoring. It was loud and annoying, but I had no concept of time, and the freedom I felt was invigorating. I drew the curtains, enabling the sun to trickle in. London was always so drab – very unlike the bright scene set before me. Yellow cabs darted about like bees collecting pollen, only the pollen was of the people kind. Waves of heat snaked along the road looking for something to engulf, and the human race was still very much on the move. Feeling hot, I pushed the old hinged window back.

"Shit! Did something die out there?"

"You'll get used to it, takes a few weeks to swallow."

I turned round, stood in my doorway, near naked and stoned, a towel rolled across his shoulders, Puk looked kind of sexy.

His shorts were far too tight, and the beads around his neck brightened his face.

"Sorry, the door was unlocked."

A half-smoked joint in his hand, brought back mixed memories. Seeing my eyes fall upon it, he handed it to me. "Welcome to the land of plenty. It's a treasure trove, baby, all you got to do is milk it." His weight shifted from left to right. "So, what brings you here?"

"Everything and nothing..." Taking a long drag I sat down. "What about you?"

"Well now that's a difficult one, 'cos most of the time I don't know my own mind." A smile crept from the corners of his mouth.

"Came for a holiday, liked the place so much I decided to stay. Ya can't get gear like this back home," he pointed to the joint, "and the women."

I raised my eyebrows.

"Well, they're just gorgeous, aren't they? Got Miss World staying here, only problem is, she's gay, but I'm working on her," a smirk left his lips, "can't be any harder than changing an engine! Anyway, I best get going before all the hot water goes. If Anna had her way, she'd dip us all like sheep once a month to save money."

He winked at me reached for his towel and left. I ditched what was left of the joint, dusted down a cassette player that the previous occupants had left and put Blondie on. I tied my hair back and began removing yesterday's makeup. Like my memories the scar on my eye had faded a bit. Wanting to forget, I smoked two fags by the window. Greasy hair and sticky skin I then set off in search of the showers.

On his way back from the showers Puk stopped and shook his hair all over me.

"There's a pie just gone in," throwing his head up he laughed, "but he'll be baked soon enough."

Not quite getting what he meant, I smiled turned left and headed towards the sound of water. Passing travellers, rusty pipes, steam and sweat all added to the pungent smell ahead.
 Soaked, and stained by the sun, the girl's face was gorgeous; high cheekbones and a chic bob, I thought she was French or Swedish.

"Bloody place never runs right!" The Scottish accent surprised me. "If Anna gets any tighter, she won't shit! And on top of that I've forgotten me shower gel!" Storming off, she stepped on a cockroach. "Filthy fuckers…!"

She rubbed her sole hard on the hall carpet and disappeared.

A tap grated, a few seconds later, hair flattened, looking like a foreign rodent an Asian emerged from behind a plastic door. Avoiding the dead cockroaches, I stepped inside. Warm water caressed me. It also washed the dead insects down the dirty plug hole. I was a million miles away when a loud banging began beating on the door.

"C'mon," it was the Scottish girl again, "I'm bloody cold

out here."

"'Old your horses"…"

Pushing the door ajar with my only free hand, I held it up for her to wait a moment.

"You bin ages! Find a good looking guy or something?"

Unable to analyse the amusement on her face, I shrugged it off with the water on my back.

"Nah, just cold water 'n' cockroaches…"

"Don't tell me it's cold after all that."

She barged past me, plonked the shower gell down and took over.

"You always this grumpy…?" I carefully eased me way out of the cubicle.

Taps on full power she poked one leg out of showering range. "Not always."

Soaping her calf, she took up a plastic razor and kicked the door shut. She was very beautiful, but had a real bite about her.

I pulled my t-shirt over my head and wandered down the hall. I think Puk had deliberately left his door ajar as he was sat inside lacing tobacco with hashish. I leaned into his doorway.

"I presume that was Miss World?"

"Ah, thought you might meet Kira. Bark's worse than her bite. Here, try this. It's good shit."

Hoarse as his voice was, he'd managed to soak the joint in saliva. I dried the end and walked towards the window where

I blew smoke into the street. Under normal circumstances, the city folk below wouldn't have been funny, but everything takes on a whole new meaning when observed through stoned eyes, and the world beneath suddenly became one big cartoon. A sea of human traffic, large brimmed hats, lots of little legs and fine frames seemed to bob and bounce all over the show. And yes, beneath those hats they did all look like pies parading around. I laughed till my sides hurt, a few minutes later and the munchies made themselves known. I watched Puk tighten his watch and pull a black shirt over his head.

"I'm going to Seven Eleven." He cocked his head to one side…"Want anything?"

"Gimmee a mo and I'll come with you!"

I wandered back to my room. Switched off my music, grabbed some dollars and locked up.

Three doors down Puk, was chatting to Kira. I wanted to start over with her, but, having had my head bitten off once, I fought against the idea and went to investigate food instead. Approaching the exit I saw Anna voicing her authority to what appeared to be the cleaner. Hands hovering like kites, her mouth and body shunted from side to side. As I neared, she replaced her sour face with a sweet one and waved the woman away.

"You sleep well, huh." Her high neck frills and fancy ways, reminded me of something royal gone wrong.

"Yeah great…"

Wanting to get away I reached for the door.

"Make sure you use my café. Speak English you know!"

"Yeah, yeah I know!"

All but a few midday moochers, the cafe empty. Still chuckling over the card game, I pulled out a chair and ordered a coffee. Sitting by the window I observed an artist across the road. He was old anyway, but too much sun made him look a hundred or so. With old wrinkly hands he struck the canvas with various blues. Every now and then the street cleared and I got a longer glimpse of his work. As a portrait of the city emerged so did my admiration for him and his art.

The waiter seemed more approachable than he had been the previous night, so I asked him for the names of some bars. 'Sat-Tines' sounded seedy, and 'Leng Moi' when translated meant 'beautiful girls,' so I settled for the 'Taverna' in the hope of pulling only pints. Taking a napkin I jotted down some directions, threw a few dollars on the table and made my way over to the old artist. He paused to smile at me before continuing to paint. Pouring the last of his heart and soul into the brush, he signed the picture. I paid him and waited for the blue boats and high rise buildings to dry before rolling and taping it up with some paper the old guy also gave me. I secured it with string and headed for the real harbour at the bottom of the hill. The sea breeze was welcome, but with it came the awful smell of engine fumes and fish. I leant over the railings watching the fishermen trying to catch whatever had the misfortune to enter their traps. Further along, I saw folks queuing for the ferry that was about to leave for Hong Kong Island opposite. As I sparked up to mask the all-pervasive smell, I heard a high-pitched squeal. Holding down a shark three fishermen cut away its fins, as if only garbage they threw the body back to sea.

"Bastards," I cussed.

"It's good soup."

A young lad smirked at my disgust. On seeing I wasn't amused, he carried his sarcasm into the crowd and disappeared.

It didn't take me long to realise there were no freebies or allowances in Hong Kong, it was simply, sink, or swim. Fighting my way through the crowds, I felt like a mouse in a maze, but kept going till my homemade map made sense. Up a side street, set slightly back, was the 'Taverna'.

I took three steps down to the entrance and went in. Inside, a small circular dance floor shone; behind it were two small decks where some DJ would work his wonders. Neatly stacked against the wall only a few stalls were in front of the bar. It was a strange sound, more like something dying than singing, so I called out. Sarcasm all over his face, a Chinese man poked his head through some beaded tassels. He tilted his head, inviting me to follow him out back. A clattering of bottles and he went back to work. I watched him make light work of his chores from between the tassels.

"I'm Pang," he put down two bottles and held out a hand, "you want to put on kettle?" Shaking my hand he pointed to a stove in the kitchen area. He wasn't stupid, knew I wanted work before I asked.

"Is quiet now, but nights are very busy." His smile became an irritating smirk, I struggled to ignore. Hoisting the crate onto an empties rack he set about making some weird looking tea.

"How much is the pay?" I sipped at my first green tea.

"Four dollar an hour…"

Before I could haggle he withdrew eye contact and began to explain how good the tips were. He was still waffling when one of the girls arrived for work.

"He's mean, huh?" Thick curly hair, olive skin and a curtly figure, I couldn't quite place the origin of the pretty girl before me.

Snapping gum, she blew and burst a bubble. Shunting forward she hung her coat and spare shoes on a hook.

"I'm Fran." She called back, "so has the old slave driver gained another force field?"

"For now …"

Apart from the annoying noise she made, she seemed ok.
Removing a shirt from a second peg, she revealed some pictures stuck to the wall. I moved closer to take a better look. A tall gaunt guy, leaning over her shoulder was pulling a silly face

"That's Jimmie." Her gum snapped again, "having lunch on Hong Kong Island with me."

"Boyfriend…?"

"Mate, his family has lived here for years. Dad's got his own business, but Jimmie prefers the puff stuff. Rebellious I suppose. So, are you starting today?"

I turned to Pang, busy observing the two of us, he removed a piece of liquorice he'd been rolling around his mouth.

"Okay. Fran show you what to do."

I followed her into the bar area where we cleaned the drip trays, bottled up, and polished glasses. She told me Pang was her uncle, not that you would ever know it if looks were anything to go by.

We were straightening the stalls when Kira entered, a pair of strappy shoes and an off the shoulder dress, she looked the bees knees.

"It's a small world, huh? Take no notice of my behaviour earlier. I'm not much good at getting up – or sharing that damn shower, especially when the water's only luke-warm."

Kira hugged Fran, changed her shoes, and headed out back where I heard Pang greet her. I didn't hear or see the DJ enter so when Booker T. & the MG's blasted out it made me jump. To begin with things were slow, but as the evening passed they speeded right up. By two in the morning I was struggling to stand the pace and every now and then took a quick breather. I was on my third break when I clocked Pang in the shadows. He had that grin on his face from earlier – the one that said I couldn't cope. I knew I was more than able; I just needed to adjust and stay awake, so when Jimmie pushed his way to the front of the bar, with the big smile I recognised from the photo, it was just what I needed to get me through my first shift.

Hook Line and Sinker

The first night at the 'Taverna' was the hardest; after that it got easier, and I got to know quite a few faces. A week had passed and it was my day off. Tired, I just wanted to chill with a beer. The 'Taverna' was quite a walk from Anna's but I convinced myself I needed the exercise more than I did a cab. The city made me feel vibrant, and on entering 'Taverna' the smell of San Miguel teased my taste buds. Ness was Swedish, and like many, had left her country to avoid ongoing and future problems. A drug deal gone wrong and she'd jumped bail before the court case, travelled across the world and got a job in a club. On the run for a string of petty crimes, she'd settled well into the city and made it her home. Her rusty hair green eyes and olive skin made her quite a catch amongst the clubs where she worked as an escort.
Like Fran, she had known Jimmie a long time and loved to smoke just about anything.

Busy talking to anyone who'd listen, Ness was all over the place when, buying a beer, I invited her to my table. We had just begun gassing girly stuff when she jumped up like a frenzied cat and ran across the empty dance floor. Bypassing Jimmie, she jumped straight into the arms of his mate. A stocky fella, full in the face but with defined features, he seemed real sure of himself.

I hadn't seen him before, but assumed they were all close by the reception received. Joining me, Jimmie helped himself to my beer.

"That's Red," he swallowed, "good mate of mine." He took a second glug at the beer, "Just back from Thailand he is." Putting the empty glass down, he burped. "Been all over the place he has."

"I can see that."

Red threw back his head of hair and lifted Ness, paying particular interest to the new silicone implants while spinning her around. He wore a blue shirt and jeans, a pair of cowboy boots too. Red was shorter than Jimmie, but then most of us were. He put Ness down and tossed his hair to one side. With one ear pierced and a tiger tattooed on his leg, he was quite a work of art. His good looks were enhanced by a piece of cut and polished jade that hung around his neck. Jimmie went behind the bar and whistled into the cellar. A few seconds later, Kira poked her head out of it. Taking up behind the bar, she eyed Red, suspicion displayed she scowled. Glancing from Red to Jimmie then back again she wiped beer spillage from her arms.

"Who's that then?"

"Get 'em in and I'll get him over." Jimmie whistled to Red and gave him a nod.

"What's up man?" Hands hovering before her boobs, he was about to inspect the new peaches.

"Cant ya see me hands are full!"

"Full of yourself," Kira turned up her nose.

Red let his deep concentration slide, standing up he swaggered over to the bar. "You got a tray?" He asked scrutinizing Kira at the same time. Kira pulled out a tray and slid it his way.

"You're not gonna wait on me then?"

"I don't wait on anyone!" Kira snapped.

No longer so sure of himself Red grunted, grabbed the tray and traipsed back to the table. Right behind him Jimmie followed. Red dished out the drinks.

"Tell us a story," Ness insisted.

"You'd ave loved Thailand this time round. Some lunatics tried to rob the elephant sanctuary. Fucked off they didn't find anything, they let the elephants out!

"Sounds awesome," Kira smiled slowly deciding to join them.

"It was, luckily they just wanted to gorge rather than roam."

"You must have been well at home then." Leaning back till the chair balanced on just two legs, Jimmie shot Red a sarcastic smile. "So tell me, did ya bring back any souvenirs?"

Before Red could answer Fran arrived, deliberately diverted his attention she twiddled his hair until it was all wrapped around her fingers.

"You back for long?" she giggled.

"You know me – here today, gone tomorrow. C'mon, this

beer's giving me gut ache. Let's roll 'n' stroll to the park."

"You're like an unsettled fly! Stay a while," Fran insisted, "I'm just about to start my shift."

"One for you, then the road," Red smiled, "then you'll have to catch us up later."

The back streets were riddled with old-timers who lived and slept on wicker recliners. Some begged for a few dollars, others, smacked out of their heads continued to let the world pass without a thought or care for it. Their brains only going to function again when the need for another hit arose. We were halfway down a second street when a sobering dodgy-looking character emerged from one of the doorways. Clocking the uncertainty on my face, Jimmie cracked one off.

"It's okay. If he thought we had anything to nick … well, it would be gone by now."

"That makes me feel *so* much better." Stood in the shadows, our on-lookers eyes followed us down the street.

"You'll get used to it," Red threw an arm around my shoulder and smirked.

"Yeah, most of them are too old to stand up – let alone get it up," Ness winked at one of the oldies.

"What're you like," Jimmie laughed, "and what's she doing…?"

Some way back Kira was cooing over kittens. Unable to understand a word she was saying the old man listening held up his hands. Kira smirked, stood up and chucked him some dollars that she hoped he would feed them with. A bit further on, we jumped down into a dry gulley crouched and crept through a tunnel. Coming out the other end we were faced with a wall either side of us. Jimmie straddled it, locking his long legs either side, he helped us up and into the park on the other side.

Tucked away and surrounded by tatty trees, the park was quite unique. Hot and humid like an army in camouflage, the trees were totally still. Dead centre was a swing to which Red raced Kira.

Shoving her to one side he seated himself snugly on it. We caught them up and sprawled on the dry grass. Being a bit of an animal, Jimmie bit the top off the beer he had brought. He downed half in one and handed the rest to Red but Red had other ideas. Jumping from the swing, he was pulling out some Thai stick, skinned-up and lit the first of many... A few joints later and I drifted off into a world of me own. As the grass took effect, his stories grew fewer and shorter. I must have slept a good hour before coming round.

"Dad's turned the spare into an office," Jimmie slurred, "so I can't help out this time round."

"If you didn't hate Hong Kong Island so much you could stay with me."

"Cheers Ness, but you know I hate it!" Red turned to us. "Don't suppose Anna's got any spare rooms?"

"Better ask her, hadn't ya?" Kira stretched as she got up.

By the time we reached Anna's I was done for. Downstairs, packed and ready to roll stood Puk. Opening our cab door he smiled…

"Great," he got in as we got out, "maybe I see you again, maybe not." He watched Red hurry towards the lift before chucking his rucksack on the back seat. A kiss on our cheeks and he was gone. Upstairs, Red was trying to negotiate with Anna. Arms crossed I found the whole thing hilarious.

"But some guy just left…." Red persisted.

"It's not clean!" Anna bleated between gritted teeth.

Red pulled out some cash to which she swiftly gave in. "You Americans all the same!" She stashed the money and smiled. "In door is key, anything else?"

"Nothing you can help with!" Red winked at her and strolled down the corridor.

With Puk gone, Red wasted no time supplying and smoking at Anna's. I don't know if Anna knew, only that she turned a blind eye to most things as long as she received her cash.

More often than not, Red was in my room. Sometimes he did stuff that surprised me, like the time I came back to find two tickets for a gig and a note next to them. "See you in Leng's at seven."

He arrived late, perspiring and breathing heavily, he chain-smoking to occupy his hands. Wiping sweat from his brow, he didn't look healthy. Trying to figure him out I frowned.

"It's just the heat." He defended ordering a double brandy that he downed in one. "C'mon, les go!"

We hurried towards the Saigon Palace. Joining a queue of

fashion freaks, we slowly bustled our way towards the entrance. Inside, bursting onto the stage screaming and strutting their stuff were 'Weather Girls. Flimsy, I watched the stage which threatened to give way under their weight. Heads swinging like chandeliers Chinese bodies crashed together. The bouncers allowed the place to fill until we were so tightly packed that the fun faded. Having had enough, I tugged at Red nodding towards the doors. He took my hand and pushed through the crowds, pass the bouncers and onto the curb where we gasped at the humid air. Hand raised he hailed a cab. Inside, he instructed the cab towards a certain street. From there we walked to the park where we collapsed under a haze of cooler air and chilled. I watched Red seal a joint. I was both surprised and grateful that he hadn't tried anything on. He was either a perfect gentleman or had a serious problem of some sort. My thoughts alongside my first tug on the joint brought on a bout of laughter. Since I could not explain myself, I was grateful when some of the others turned up.

"They may be short and fat," Kira shouted. "But boy, they know how to play."

"Didn't know you guys were gonna be there," Red queried.

Kira smoothed her silk dress over her hips and smiled. "Girl gotta shake a real bootie now and then."

"Too right," Fran agreed, smiling as she shuffled a pack of cards. "C'mon, Red, you're always up for the kill. How much you got on ya?"

"Not a lot and you know I won't play without a wad of me own."

"Wanker," Fran joked, "Just don't like losing, do you?"

"Who does?" Red had just settled back down when Jimmie turned up.

"Deal us in," he shouted to Fran. Accompanied by two feminine lads none of us had ever met before, Jimmie moved closer. Fran jumped up and smiled.

"Wow, what I'd give for a wiggle like that!"

There was no hiding their gay status, the walk, the wiggle, the smooth skin and girly smiles that were more feminine than most of us.

"I'll have the hips." Ness slid across the grass, inviting the gorgeous boys to sit either side of her.

Having just scored some Thai stick from Jimmie, they put one together and watched the first game. After one bad hand, I gave it up. I wasn't that good, and needed what cash I had to get by. My withdrawal presented an opportunity for the new lads who asked to be dealt in. Kira shuffled the cards and dealt them out. Peeking at the cards Ness held Red encouraged her to up the stakes on the last few hands. Pissed at losing to a bird, the gays gave Red a foul look and hissed to one another in Cantonese. They then grabbed their gear and tobacco and disappeared back into town. Jimmie, who'd thrown in more than he should have, sulked over his loss before lifting his head to stare at Kira who was sitting cross-legged in some kind of Buddhist stance. Another bad loser, she pressed her lips together and clicked her nails.

"It's just a bloody game." Ness smiled putting away the best part of $500. "Who gives a shit...?" There was silence. "C'mon, you lot. Shame that Chink is the other way, been giving him the eye all night. Am I not more appealing than his mate's backbone?" Ness tried to break the atmosphere but her joke failed to break the silence, so I did.

"Better to have a handful of dollars than a fistful of bent bollocks."

Kira gave me one of her shifty looks quickly followed by one of her unpredictable smiles. A few minutes later, Fran jumped up and startled us all.

"I think we need to change the scenery. C'mon, let's go down the beach, we can crash a while then have a swim. There's a mobile take-out that comes by if we get hungry."

Red got straight on his feet and fumbled for cab change. A few minutes later, we were all rolling towards one of the bays. I was surprised at how much sand lay on the beaches; for some reason, I thought it was going to be real rocky. We paid off the cab, kicked off our shoes, and ran onto the beach. Squashing gritty parcels of sand between our toes, waddling like ducks we must have looked hilarious to any onlookers. Pulling all sorts of weird faces, Jimmie looked pretty mad. Finally making it to the beach shrubs, the sound of the waves relaxing, it didn't take long for us to fall asleep. Just as Fran had hoped, the smell of fresh grub woke us. Following new tracks across the sand, I went with her to the portable food cabin.

A funny-looking little man selling chips and all sorts of fried fish served us several portions of cod, crab, and chips that we carried back. Everyone was awake except for Red, who appeared to be in some sort of coma, so we left him to it and shared what there was.

"Try this…" Fran speared a piece of octopus and held it in front of me.

I couldn't face it, so I passed it to Jimmie, who had no problem chewing the blistered rubber.

Full and feeling hot, I stripped down to my underwear and ran towards the refreshing sea. Bobbing away, I lay on my back drifting until the waves were no more than a faint surge below, and the sun a sheet of shiney glass. It was Kira's voice that brought me back. I used my hand to block the sun's glare and flipped over. She was quite a long way from where I had drifted, but her voice reached me.

"You're too far out! Jimmie reckons there are giant jellies and sharks!"

Endless water behind and below that fucking film jaws sprang to mind. There were no fins on the horizon, but a large sponge, followed by some smaller ones floating towards me. Freaked out, fear had me swimming faster than usual, overtaking Kira I didn't stop till my feet felt sand and I was standing up again. Catching me up Kira and I found ourselves face-to-face with two police officers. Their eyes never rose above our boobs – not even when they spoke.

"No nudity," the first barked.

"That's right!"

The second shook a skinny finger in the air before pointing to the rest of the gang who apart from Red were fast pulling wet t-shirts over their heads and waving furiously in our direction. I glanced down at my transparent underwear and couldn't help laughing.

"Surely they're not serious?"

"I think they are," Kira said, watching the first officer fondled the cuffs hanging from his belt.

"Okay," she went on, "we get the picture."
I could feel them watching us all the way back till we reached the group.

"Those guys are seriously fucked up," Jimmie hissed.

"No boobs on beach," Ness shrieked, "bloody hypocrites, this city fucks like thunder all night!"

"Well, that was educational." I walked to where Red was still snoozing and kicked some sand over his feet. "Didn't fancy it then?"

"Nah, I'm a sun soaker." He stretched like a starfish and buried his arms under a thin layer of sand.

"Suit yourself." I stepped over him and sat down near Ness.

"I know a place that'll suit you." Red sat up, wiping the sand from his shirt and legs. "I heard the DJ down the 'Junction' is real cool, much better than the last one."

Jimmie looked at him, "Good, then we'll all get going down there later."

Red smiled to himself and dusted the remainder of the sand from his legs. The rest of the day dragged, I think a combination of being stoned, tired and hungry kinda has that effect on you.

The 'Junction' was a large underground club managed by two bouncers one of whom Red greeted warmly.

"Thai my man, how ya doing?"

Taller than any other Chinese I had seen Thai towered above us all. Clean shaven he wore an impressive tailor made suit. "Go ahead guys," Red waved us all on, "I'll catch ya in a minute."

The entrance to the club was dark, after that it brightened and opened up into a pretty smart pad. The place was covered in vines, trees and stuffed animals. Had it still been dark the place could have easily been mistaken for a real jungle and some of the many people there the animals. On the way to the bar the girls spotted an empty alcove and grabbed it. Knowing he couldn't carry the whole order, Jimmie asked me to lend a hand. He stopped at the end of the bar and pulled me towards him.

"So, how d'ya like the city so far?"

"It's different; pretty wild, I suppose all these are real?"

"Who…?"

"The animals, you plum…!"

"Oh yeah, yeah they are." Giving his order, Jimmie then

pointed to a gorilla above the bar. "Doesn't look too happy, does he?"

"Neither would you if someone shoved a hose up your arse, and shot it full of foam."

Having just taken a swig of beer, Jimmie couldn't help but shower the floor with it. Still laughing, "that was good, Sharm, I like that."

"Bet they don't!" I shot the gorilla one last glance, relieved him of three vodkas and joined the girls. Having removed a small turtle from the back wall, Kira was trying to figure out how they stuffed something so small.

"They do it all by hand." From the shadows appeared Red. He took one of the beers from Jimmie and downed it in one, took the turtle from Kira, hung it back up, and was gone again. Feeling good after a few drinks, we made for the dance floor. By midnight, we'd worked hard for Madonna and I was feeling hungry. Ness wasn't ready to go, pissed she hung back with some people she knew. Tired of waiting for Red, I left with Kira and Jimmie, who insisted we try a real Chinese take-away. There were loads of fast-food places along the way, but none I really fancied.

Most of the meat looked like something the dog had thrown up, or, worse still, probably *was* the dog, but Jimmie insisted it wasn't all bad. Against my better judgement, we agreed to try something and entered one of the shops. We approached the counter where Jimmie had ordered a variety of tasters. We'd just sat down when a huge guy took over the table opposite us, his chin was so folded in surplus flesh, that it grew and shrank each time he opened his mouth. He dunked drummers as though swatting flies and continued to fill his face.

"If you look at him, you'll never eat anything!" With this remark, Jimmie changed places to blot him out and put several fried potatoes on my plate.

"Veggie dish ain't bad." Kira offered us some of what she had.

We were doing okay till Jimmie went for round two and came back with pork and beef balls. I chewed for a moment before spitting out a lump of gristle. One further look at the fat guy was all I needed to give it up completely.

"You've no sense of adventure," Jimmie mumbled through a full mouth.

I gave what I had left to a stray dog and shook my head.

"I'll stick to tins if you don't mind. Least I know what's in em."

We walked back to Anna's, where we retired to my room to skin-up. I heard Red's footsteps before he arrived, pleased to see him I sat up, but Jimmie was way ahead of me and on his feet within seconds. Red, removed a bag of cocaine from his pocket, waved it about like some sort of sacred flag, then sat at the dressing table and started to empty it out. Now up and about, Kira hovered over him. I felt tired, trapped, and confused. Bad energy was pouring in like a plague. 'No,' was repeating itself over and over again in my brain, but curiosity had silenced my vocal chords. I mean for fuck sake it was only a tiny bit of white powder? I'd hear loads of stories about cocaine but in truth hadn't got a clue. Ness's sudden arrival brought a moment's normality until.

"Had to hang about, make sure Thai came up with the goodies."

"More like you were being nosey!"

"Shut up Red and get on with it!"

Not quite what I'd planned I wanted the ground to open up. It wasn't new to her or the others – they'd all done it at some point before, and didn't see what the big deal was. Red had the gift of the gab, going on about how irresistible the buzz was. At one point, he reminded me of a good salesman that you give in to just to shut him up. While he crushed diamond-like powder all over the cabinet, I stared in silence, wondering what could be so dangerous about something so beautiful. I sat down next to him and rubbed it between my fingers.

"Hurts your nose, don't it?"

"Yeah, so we won't go there."

Confused, I creased my forehead. Red fumbled inside his jacket and quickly pulled out a handful of syringes and a large spoon. Rolling up his sleeve for the first time, I saw it was a mess.

"It's the best way, if ya wanna fly." I turned to hear the words bursting from Jimmie's mouth. "A little here and there never hurt no-one," he continued.

"Let's cut the crap!" Ness sniped. "We've waited long enough for this."

She paced the room as though her feet were on fire, lighting her third fag. Jimmie sat on the bed and pulled a belt around his arm, before jacking up he paused.

"It's only a dabble, it's too expensive to do regularly," he assured me, "which makes it a bit of a pleasure."

Tightening his belt, he took a syringe from Red, and as if doing nothing more than shaving, shot himself up. I took my eyes away from him while I watched Ness help Kira before injecting herself.

"That's fucking wicked!" Needle still in his arm, Jimmie fell back on the bed. Ness collapsed next to him like a deflated balloon, and snaked her arms around Kira's waist. I should have just walked out, but in that moment, my legs were as weak as the rest of me, and it looked like they were having a good time. Red rolled up my sleeve.

"Don't worry, you'll love it."

The needle hurt as he pushed it in. I watched the clear liquid disappear into my veins.

I felt nothing at first, just a toxic smell that surged through every sensor until it reached my tongue. Then, without warning, a thunderbolt exploded, surging through my body like an uncontrollable tidal wave, it gathered momentum.

Then, without warning it shattered in a million different directions. It was the ultimate adrenaline rush that disintegrated faster than fast. As the fleeting fireworks left my mind my stomach muscles threatened to eject my intestines through my mouth. Knowing I had no control, I ran to the toilet and joined Kira who too was struggling for vomit that didn't exist. As sweat became cold, so panic converted itself, allowing paranoia to set in like rigor mortis. It was like I had an unbearable disease that could only be cured by feeding its craving with more cocaine. Since I had no knowledge of downers, I took myself up again and again. We all did, until there was nothing left. When the gear ran out, so did everyone else. Red turned the coke wrappers inside out and cleaned the spoon over and over again, refusing to give up. I could hear Kira banging about in her room, every now and then she'd pop her head round my door, light a fag and disappear again. Taking himself into the bathroom, Red did one last hit, after that he had no trouble finding sleep. I scrabbled amongst the smokes on the side and burned hash that crumbled everywhere except into the tobacco it was meant for. Smoking it didn't make a dent in my desire for more cocaine or my circular one brain. Kira stopped pacing from room to room and eventually settled next to me. It was the early hours of the morning before mental exhaustion forced us both to sleep. Like a zombie I crawled through the day, only one thing on my mind I needed that feeling back again. In seven eleven I bought a bottle of whisky but it did nothing to simmer the irritation and craving for more. Watching Red wake up was like the sun rising.

After that, every night was one big party that always ended

in a non-communicative come-down. It took less than a week for the bruising to darken. My arms weren't just yellow or blue – they were as black as the ace of spades. Great big unsavoury blotches stained them from wrist to elbow. Cocaine had become our only concern, and all our personalities had changed overnight. It wasn't a dabble as expressed by Jimmie, it was a giant net that we were all caught up in.

There is no intermission with cocaine. Its moods are ruthless, frivolous and senseless, its character conceited, cocky, and irrational. With its unsatisfied hunger and unquenchable thirst, cocaine is constantly searching for victims.

The new habit created so much paranoia, I found myself depressed and mentally exhausted and nothing in the world extinguished it, accept cocaine. Sleep rarely came, and when it did, it brought its worst nightmares whether night or the day. I became nothing but a zombie, living my own personal nightmare. I would light a cigarette and look in the mirror. Hardly recognizable, my eyes were ingrained with dark circles. It had only been a few weeks, but it felt like an eternity.

We'd become adrenaline freaks overnight, rushing through time as a black hole rushes through space. We were getting through several grams a night and time wasn't stopping for anything. I couldn't inject myself, but Red had no problem with it. Watching him feel his way through my bruises made me feel sick. My arms were really sore, so I turned away and bit my lip. I was unable to face work, so gave it up, as did Kira, shortly afterwards. Desperately addicted, I used the last of my emergency savings, till they, too, were gone.

Lack of sleep was slowly sending me mad. I had forgotten what it felt like. Nothing calmed the poisons or tamed the frustration running through my bloodstream. My polluted body pounded under sweat-drenched covers, tossing and turning, ready to explode. Red slept too well for my liking, so I confronted him demanding to know his secret.

"It's heroin, okay? I didn't want ya to start using cos you'll never get off it."

"It's a bit fucking late for all that," I screamed, "now line it up before I go properly mad."

Without considering the consequences or anything else I was focused on one thing only. Coming down from the cruel permanent pain in my head and body, making the paranoia go away, the sweats dry up and sew my mind back together.

I snorted heaps of the stuff. Like magic all my pains went away, I stopped sweating and shaking, Instead of paranoia I was on top of the world, numb and unafraid. A bitter sweet taste secreted my throat, a suddenly heat it surged through my bones and into my head. Feeling on top of the world, I threw my arms around Red and found myself thanking him for the very thing he'd got me into. And so I became a slave to the most evil poison on the planet.

Polished Brass

I had often seen the lights for a club called 'China City' I'd also heard the girls mention it from time to time. Because I now had a serious cash problem, I began to play with camouflage. It was my first makeover in weeks, and I struggled to come to terms with the state of myself.

I put foundation over my arms to hide the mess, but nothing was going to cover the ghastly colours displayed there. I stopped en route at a designer boutique and purchased a pair of long-sleeved gloves that would have been pretty trendy had they not been hiding the evidence of my lifestyle.

The cab pulled up outside a tall building that housed the famous club. Inside, a doorman watched as I pondered over which of four lifts to take. I was getting flustered when he pointed at one. The lift stopped with a small jolt and the doors opened. As I stepped out, I entered a whole new world, the world of sleaze and glamour.

Sophisticated women floated around, preparing themselves for whatever events the evening held. Bouncers busied themselves chatting to pretty girls, while a band polished its brass, ready to rock the huge dance floor set before me. Middle-aged women in suits flew about the place displaying their impatience and frustration. It was like being at Old Trafford football stadium, only the players were all well-dressed women ready to boot another kind of ball. Diamond spotlights embedded throughout the ceilings created universal light that enhanced satin drapes and velvet seats. Overwhelmed by my glamorous surroundings, I almost forgot why I was there, until a stunning Chinese woman approached. Hair twisted into a small ball, it was held in place by lethal-looking chopstick. She held out a slender hand with immaculate nails and introduced herself as Honey, better known as the Canton Queen. She then led the way to the boss. In a back room, she introduced me to designer-dressed Eddie Wong. Smug, but only too happy to offer employment, he led me to the makeup room, where he introduced, Sassy Chang, who sat me down and explained the house rules, be good, look good, and drink like a goldfish. It was a high-class hooker joint that was going to take care of all my bad habits, for a price, of course.

With the torture of withdrawal on the horizon, I began immediately, and so did the long journey of want and waste. Thanks to heroin feelings and emotions became a thing of the past, and dealers and dollars the new craze. The conversation of the clientele bored me senseless, which accounted for my liquid intake of Regal.

'China City' owned a string of hotels just a few miles away, where we collected the real cash. There was always some kind of new speculation floating around, like the girl who'd been found dead after a heated debate with some guy from hell, but business and addiction stopped at nothing. My lungs sometimes flapped about my chest like an injured bird, but addiction was an expensive habit, one I could no longer afford without large sums of money. Torn between the two evils, I simply increased my heroin habit until everything inside me seemed to die.

Sometimes the evenings were spiced up by eccentric punters throwing dinner parties on their yachts in the harbour. One in particular needed careful attention and that's where Honey and I came in. During the briefing, we were told that he was as fussy as he was rich, but, if we played our cards right, we would have a lot of money. The posh party sounded great compared with the normal mundane carry-on. All we had to do was dress up, dine, and dance all night. With all the arrangements taken care of, Honey invited me on a shopping spree. It wasn't something I did often due to my powerful addictions, but I did need some new clothes, so I agreed to meet her. I hadn't been inside any of the plazas and had a great time whizzing around. Honey tried everything from suits to swimwear. Each time Honey entered the changing rooms, I found myself searching for stuff that would cover my arms. My dress of the day was a yellow quarter-length with purple spots.

By the end of the afternoon, our bellies were as full as our shopping bags. The cab dropped me at my road, and Honey arranged to meet me in the club lobby by seven. As I entered the bedsit, Anna kept me chatting so that she could peek over the tops of my shopping bags. Sensing her inquisitiveness, I tossed her one of the silk scarves I'd bought. I knew she liked it by her facial expression in fact she was so pleased, that she followed me down the hall and handed the new arrivals a bar of soap before I complained about the smell they had brought with them. As I passed Kira's room, I knocked but she was out. I heard Red snoring before I entered my room. Leaving him to it, I got ready and left to meet Honey. The crushed velvet dress she wore complimented her figure beautifully. We had just lit cigarettes when a posh figure entered the club, paused in the doorway and smiled.

Harry Valentine spoke proper English and had a nose that flew higher than Concorde. He reminded me of a preserved pug dog. He had so many creases in his forehead, a bit like the old trees in the park, and I imagined each and every one probably had a great sanctimonious story to tell. After a quick handshake, he led us to his Mercedes. Inside, a player oozed an operatic soundtrack that made my ears cringe. Realising it was irritating me he began a lecture on the beauty of it. As I was unable to grasp it, I rummaged around in my bag and handed him the latest Madonna cassette.

He grudgingly exchanged it, pushing it in as though it had the lurgy or something. A few minutes later, he let his guard down and began humming to *Holiday*. More interested in grooming herself, it didn't bother Honey either way. I caught her eye in the small mirror above me; smoothing herself like a

Persian cat, she returned the smile.

The harbour wasn't far; two songs later, we could hear mixed music emanating from the many boats there.

I needed no clues as to which one belonged to Harry. The *Valentine* outclassed everything else in size and quality. The faint sounds of Abba seeped through its bow and a chauffeur waited to take the car. Leading the way Harry began walking the posh plank. Two bouncers held the boarding ramp still as we wobbled up it. Inside, a string of pompous winge-bags began kissing arse. My head bobbed up and down in silent greetings whilst my brain absorbed the fashion, furs and fixtures all around me.

More interested in Harry's gadgets than his many false friends, I lit a cigarette and went to look for an ashtray. I peered over the swing doors which divided the yacht and saw one sitting on a glass sheet held up by a carved elephant. Leaving the geese to gabble, I made my way over to it. Harry had many unique items dotted about the ship, hanging on the wall an African face released ice on the touch of its nose, a glass eagle in the corner shone brightly through blue-studded eyes, but my favourite thing had to be the table. I knelt down in order to observe the elephant more clearly and was miles away when I was rudely interrupted.

"Isn't it divine; you know, the peasants down town carve them all by hand, takes forever, but it's all they know."

Like the screw heels in her shoes, her voice was quite cutting, and the leather suit failed to contain the rolls of fat clinging around her middle. On the contrary, it looked like someone had painted it there, and the real fur collar confirmed her to be every bit the bitch that she was.

"And I suppose they get paid mere peanuts for all their efforts?"

"Peasants and peanuts," the sentence pleased her, "what a great catchphrase."

She had a smile that mocked everything in its path, and her arrogance was boring.

"And what do you do that's so artistic?" I asked her, tongue in cheek.

She didn't answer, just stood examining the triangular tips of her shoes with a devious smile. Rather than argue, I headed back to Honey who handed me a glass of champagne.

"Bottoms up," she gurgled. "It's the only way to deal with 'em."

Taking the flute from her, I examined a portrait that hung above one of the exits. Three thoroughbreds were about to leap out of the picture when the bitch from hell jumped through the door instead.

"Harry, darling, how are you?" She looked pointedly at me, then Honey, "you *have* been busy and you've mixed them just like your drinks."

A half-smile and Harry introduced the monster to us.

"Claudia is an old friend of mine. We go back a long way."

The word 'old' hung in the air like a bad smell. Twice my age and more, Claudia was clearly irritated by the remark. In a desperate attempt to erase his error, Harry called for more champagne and handed out cigarettes like sweets. Honey, struggling to keep a straight face, pulled out a Chinese fan and hid behind it. The only one available I bore the brunt of her temper.

"In answer to your question back there," she snapped, "my art is fashion," she glanced at my dress. "I must say that those spots are rather overrated outdated even."

I was getting hot and bothered, but my cardigan was hiding my arms, so I couldn't very well remove it. Though the thought of what her face would look like if she saw the bruises was quite amusing, I lowered my eyes towards her bumpy bottom.

"I think your fox collar would be better around your middle. Let it hang like a tail then you can chase yourself … aye."

Honey put the fan away and headed for the ladies. She had a lovely figure that she wiggled from side to side as she moved. Trying to hide her envy and jealousy, Claudia watched in disgust. She was as transparent as cling film, and played hardball in order to win the jackpot, but Harry played his own games in his own field. I waited for Honey to reappear, and I motioned for her to join me on the dance floor, as it seemed to be the safest option to escape the sarcastic bitch. I closed my eyes, only opening them to remove the odd hand that wandered onto the floor after us.

Three songs later, the music stopped and a banquet of

silver service was presented from behind closed curtains. Seats were allocated, and everything was cool until the waiters wheeled in a tank of live lobsters. It was just the start of something awful, and watching them clamber about made me feel ill.

"Why do they stare like that?" I asked.

Honey was about to answer when the English earwig Claudia interfered.

"Because darling you're going to eat it." Barking loud enough for everyone to hear, she ogled her audience. Instead of rising to her remark, I simply drank more champagne and tried to keep the conversation to just Honey. Claudia was annoyed at my whispering and deliberately asked the waiter to wheel the trolley of lobster over to her.

"Are they gonna boil 'em?" I asked Honey.

"Of course, but first we choose which we want." Claudia just couldn't help herself.

"Well, you can count me out!" I snapped for the first time.

"Don't be sentimental!" Harry moaned. "Would you prefer food poisoning?"

I was going off Harry and his harem of desperados faster than fast. It was okay for him – he was a regular fixture in Chinese society. Honey had been born and bred in the city, and Claudia had climbed enough ropes to know them all. The conversation quickly became a heated debate on how to kill a lobster without boiling the fucker to death. I knew I wasn't going to win the argument, so I decided to become a temporary vegetarian. Annoyed at their attitudes, I left my order of rice noodles on the table and headed off for a quick sniff in the loo.

On the way back, I passed Harry's bedroom; the door was wide open revealing all sorts of luxuries. The wardrobes had giant brass handles that I just had to pull on. The inside was full of silks and satins made to the highest standard. Designer suits and satin slippers filled the available space. I ran my hand down one of the dresses. Claudia's name met my fingers at the bottom.

Harry's hobbies were outrageous, and Claudia was a mug for allowing it, but it still didn't excuse her bad manners. She had a mouth on her, and I could still hear her commanding and demanding as I headed back. I hesitated in the doorway before re-joining them. I wanted to walk out but needed the money to survive. When I returned, I saw that the lobster had been cooked and they were all busy eating it. Pushing a plate of shells my way, Claudia deliberately smiled.

"Umm, that was an adorable appetizer."

I was beginning to feel irritable. Harry, like everyone else, was getting drunker by the minute; leaning across the table he began to grope me and Honey openly. I was grateful for the arrival of the main course, as it gave his hands a second occupation, but as one irritation stopped, so another began.

"Is that a natural tan or one of those annoying birthmarks?"

I looked up from my noodles to find Claudia firing again.

"Pigment," I blurted, "how about yours?"

"Christian Dior, darling..."

I felt a foot pressing upon mine from under the table. I scanned the faces of the people close enough to reach and found Honey smiling at me. She winked and blew a silent 'fuck 'er' from her bottom lip, but it was easier said than done. I was tired of listening to Claudia's bullshit when her mouth wasn't full.

Having finished his meal, Harry continued his small talk with the business boys who were all trying to get into his bag. Flitting from me to Honey, round the table at the Japanese, and back again to us, Claudia struggled to keep her eyes still. Bored, she continued to dig with her invisible shovel. This time she addressed Harry.

"So where did you say you met the girls?" Harry didn't hear her the first time, so she repeated herself twice as loudly.

"City," Harry snapped.

My blood was beginning to boil, and the inside of my cheek was getting chewed. Seeing my anger, Harry changed the subject from shares to antiques in the hope that I would be interested. He told me about a car he'd purchased on Peng Chau a remote island not too far away, but Claudia refused to be left out.

"It never did work properly, did it, darling?" Suggesting she'd had a hand in purchasing the posh wheels, Claudia beamed from ear to ear, followed it through with a hair ruffle; she then shuffled closer to Harry.

"It was old, hadn't been fired up for years," he snapped.

"Bit like her, then," I stared straight at Claudia as I took command of the table. "You know, I've just realized something, 'Arry. We've got something in common after all."

"There's a word," Claudia mumbled to her Asian neighbour, but the table now belonged to me.

"My dad use to collect birds like Claudia every weekend. They were all over-filthy, well-used, and way past their sell-by dates. He'd have been better off with a lapdog; they're much cheaper than old charmers like her."

"How dare you! You're all the same, you girls. How's anyone supposed to tell you lot apart"

Honey stood up and took the lead.

"For a start, Sharm's collars and cuffs don't match, and if you're as dry between the sheets as your humour is, well, it explains why we're here, doesn't it!"

"What is this 'collar cuffs'?" The Jap next to Harry turned to him for an answer.

Harry looked as though he'd been stuffed into a blender and was ready to embrace orbit with a rocket full of embarrassment. Since voicing an opinion would only start an argument, Harry lit a cigarette and tried to keep his guard up. While the intriguing and amusing whispers flew around the table, Honey raised her glass and finished her drink. She turned away from the table and headed to the nearest exit where she waited for me. I grabbed a plastic tiara from a table decoration on my way over to her and placed it on her head.

"There, now you're a real Canton Queen."

She adjusted the crown and smiled. The conversation at the table had run dry, and, since it had been his team who'd started the fray, Harry would have to accept an embarrassing defeat.

White Lights
I Would Die for You

The large pay packet that Harry Valentine personally delivered, along with an apology, did nothing but help expand my addictions. My room became a circle of sessions for anyone who wanted to fly. Some nights there were so many of us going up, we couldn't even see one another through the smoky air. More drugs seemed to enter my room than dollars at the club downtown. Sleeping it off all day was the usual form before scoring, shooting, and sniffing all over again. What a fucking existence!

For some unknown reason, we always injected cocaine and snorted heroin. Why, I don't know, that's just how it was.

I had lost track of time and its meanings until Jimmie turned up in a red Santa suit. Waving and spraying a can of snow he covered me, the mirror and then Red who as always was asleep. Waking to the sound of compressed air, Red sat up.

"Fuck, man, shame the stuff ain't real."

"Christ, is that all you ever think about?" Jimmie was on one, and impatient. He occasionally had outbursts of energy when he wasn't at home sleeping off a low.

"You up for some festive fun then or not…?"

Jimmie jumped onto the bed, bouncing while singing *Merry Christmas Everyone*; I wasn't too sure about the 'everybody's having fun' bit, because it felt more like something out of the fucking film, 'Merry Christmas Mr Laurence!' I wrapped a cardigan around my shoulders and looked out of the window.

"Yeah, why not…? Let's escape before the night shift arrives."

Red was still under the duvet, so I pushed him onto the floor and with Jimmie frosted his hair and socks. Moving the fastest he had in a long time Red tried to wriggle away. By the time we'd finished, he looked like a badger, shook himself down, dunked his face in the sink and grabbed a coat. No party was complete without Kira, so we banged on her door. Two knocks later, a classy Thai girl opened it. Seeing things were about to rock, she got her belongings and left. Fingers tapping the door, Jimmie eyed the firm arse, and champagne hips as they disappeared down the hall.

"Not bad," he trailed off. "Not bad at all."

"You," Kira chuckled, "referring to me or her?"

"Either," Jimmie said shutting his jaw. "Don't know how you do it, what you got that I ain't?"

"D'ya, really want me to answer that?" Kira smirked.

By the time we reached McDonalds there had been so many different comments made that Jimmie accidentally asked for a tit burger. Setting the waitress straight, he tried to be more serious. Still laughing, we sat beside the window and watched the outside world. We counted pie-faces until Ness and Fran broke the Chinese cycle. Coming towards us, Fran looked like an Asian alien, the bobbles on her dress flashing and wobbling as she walked. Ness had dyed her hair pink and backcombed it into a mass of candy floss. Outside they squashed their faces against the glass making ugly prints while entertaining us. Finished eating, we joined them and walked to the pub, where we ordered brandies that we hoped would warm us all up.

We didn't inject cocaine that night, just snorted it at every opportunity, but it wasn't the same. As the night disappeared, we grew quiet and miserable, going back to Anna's we slept. I awoke around lunchtime squashed between Kira and Jimmie, whose long hair was stuck to my face. I brushed it away, and sat up. Jimmie had sprayed 'Happy Christmas' across the mirror more than once, but a sense of gloom had crept in during the night consuming the festive season. It wasn't how Christmas was meant to be, but it was mine.

Red stirred from the sofa, looking rattled and rough. He asked me to pass him a magazine that he straightened enough to crush heroin on. As soon as he began to prepare gear, Jimmie got up to go. He didn't do heroin – just occasionally stuck a needle of coke in his arm for a quick fix. Drugs were drugs, but Jimmie had weird ways. As I stuffed the note up my nose, I caught his eye. There I detected a glimpse of guilt. Seconds later, the door closed and he was gone, taking any Christmas spirit with him.

It was the worst festive season ever, and, as numb as I felt, somewhere deep down, a small part of me cried out for the normality of Christmas. I longed to be the little kid with the long strands of hair trailing down her back, the kid who'd danced in the rain without a care in the world. The kid who had made her own entertainment and made do. There hadn't been much in my house, but even Dad's moaning seemed like heaven compared with this. The bells of wrong were ringing out, but I could do nothing to stop my addiction. Just like a bully, it had wormed its way into my system, worked out all my weaknesses, and run me into the ground.

As I sat up, I exchanged stories of Christmas past with Red and Kira. After a while, we ran out of stuff to say and became expressionless. I knew that I'd completely lost the plot so there was nothing left to do but snort myself to sleep.

I was awakened by a recurring dream that soon became reality. I could feel an army of tiny feet running back and forth across the bed. Scared shitless, I drew my hands under the old covers. My stomach churned as the creatures scampered to and fro. I reached out for Kira, but she had done one. I shifted across the mattress and felt for Red, but he was out cold. Frozen with fear, my own sweat nearly suffocated me. Eventually, I drifted off to the beat of my own heart. Red must have drawn the curtains, because I awoke to light streaming in through the dirty window. On hearing him in the bathroom, I jumped up.

"Did you feel 'em?"

"Who, what…?"

"The rats…"

"Didn't feel a thing, but it wouldn't surprise me."

"Wouldn't surprise you, what d'ya mean wouldn't surprise you?"

"There's food dumped around every restaurant in town. Some places even serve 'em up if they run out." Red wasn't bothered one bit.

"Great, so we're sharing a room with fucking rats! Why don't we just move into the sewers and save ourselves a few quid, put their favourites on the fucking shopping list!" I shoved a takeaway onto the floor. "Why not just jack em up, invite em to join the pissin party!" Clothes in need of a good wash or iron littered the room. Bins overflowed with butts and used needles. Sat on the cabinet, plastic cups with mould growing in them stood to attention. I threw a plastic cup at Red. "It's a fucking shit 'ole. We can't stay 'ere with rats!"

I grabbed my jeans, stormed out and headed to the harbour front where I found a letting agency. Extremely expensive, apartments weren't cheap in the concrete city, in fact, they were like gold dust. I'd have to work a month just to raise a deposit, and that was without the addiction in tow. The others didn't know how much Harry had given me, fortunately I'd put some in the bank. I was weeks away from anything remotely close to the advertised figures, but something about owning a bankbook actually made me feel better about the whole situation.

Since I didn't want to go back, I made an early entrance at the club. I spent most of my time in a recliner reading an old magazine that one of the girls had left; by five the place got busier and I needed to get changed. There was stuff in my locker that I'd long forgotten; taking one of the dresses I redid my make up and asked to be allocated a table. The glamour of 'China City' replaced the four-legged rats with the suited and booted ones. The species was the same – just the surroundings were different. I drank my way through a whole bottle of brandy while I tried to seem interested in the global currency being discussed. At the end of it all I was desperate for a long line of something hard to alleviate the blues so I headed for home.

I knew something was wrong as soon as I walked in. Anna sat in her chair discreetly waving her hands from side to side. The desk was scattered with a variety of passports and the moneybox was upside down.

"Routine check," she whispered to me.

It was a relief to know that I had no gear on me, but I had hoped to get some.

"Red…?" I asked, hoping she had an answer.

"I don't know. They come quickly."

"Never knew I had so many neighbours," I murmured, seeing all the unfamiliar faces being pushed from inside their rooms out. An American girl exercised her rights as the cops emptied her pockets. Two Swedes lay face down fighting the cuffs police wrapped around their arms, and an Indian girl burst into tears as she was taken out. They had Kira, but she seemed to be enjoying the female frisk till they found half a joint in her room and detained her. I didn't know what to do. I couldn't help Kira, so I turned to leave, but an officer on his way in grabbed me. I felt my hands begin to tingle as I was pushed down the hall towards my personal part of the world. As we got closer two more officers joined the one behind me.

"This room yours?"

Kicking the broken door ajar, one of them poked his head inside and pulled me up beside him. Someone must have been rummaging, because the bed was littered with underwear and stockings, and there was a mountain of heels on the floor; as I saw the mess I began to laugh.

"Unless Red's a transvestite, then, yeah, it's my room."

"Is funny... He wears knickers, huh?"

The officer tightened the cuffs in temper.

"It's a joke, ha ha – get it?"

"Is American, huh?"

Disappointed by the tone in his voice, I nodded.

"One of the first to go. Had something he should not."

As I turned to face him, I saw his smile exaggerate until it could go no further across his face.

"Been detained, destined for local magistrates in the morning – get the picture?"

Desperate to get the cuffs off, I nodded. They checked my passport for validation and searched my belongings. With nothing on me, they left me in the mess they had made. I sat on the bed for ages before wandering along the littered hall to see Anna. As the last officer left, she tore a Chinese fan from the wall and waved it under her chin. A nagging pain I'd never experienced before was beginning to emerge in my head, my legs felt heavy, and a wave of exhaustion passed over me, forcing uncontrollable yawns. I needed gear, and, if my twinge was anything to go on, so would Red and Kira by morning.

I'd never had to score by myself, but had often heard that Chung King Mansion, was a good place for gear, it was home to many, but mostly those who took drugs. Getting a cab was easy, getting out was harsh. The smell of contamination and corruption was pure and potent. Sacks of rubbish piled either side of the entrance festered, while people bustled in and out like mice. Inside, old-timers sat in the shadows. I couldn't see what they were doing, but recognized the smell of heroin as they burnt it. I felt myself being watched. With so many dodgy and desperate faces to choose from, I found my feet glued to the ground. My headache was becoming increasingly painful so, when a lanky character nodded to me, I went for it and scored all I could afford.

My skin began to crawl on top of my jittering bones, cold and clammy I hurried to the first public toilet I could find. I tore the bag open so fast that my soggy fingers struggled to crush the rocks of heroin. The urgency to feel better was so strong that I ended up snorting abrasive rocks, powder, and all. After three lumpy lines I came up for air, and my internal heaters kicked in, warming my body from head to toe. And with that, back came my confidence. I wrapped up the remaining rocks and walked back to Anna's.

I bumped into Jimmie along one of the main drags. He was drunk, but insisted on buying tea and coffee. He told me that the law did routine busts quite often, leaving things a few months then repeating them. Since the law had already been, Jimmie said Anna's was the safest place to be and insisted on keeping me company till morning court. The coffee had little effect on the beer which was swimming round his system and he chatted till the early hours while I half-listened.

My ears were still ringing when we arrived at the courts the next morning. Sitting cross-legged on the floor, Chinese prisoners looked on with distant stares. Others sat or stood above and behind them; among those standing was Red. Confidence replaced by torment, his perspiration dripped onto the heads below him. Breathing in the hope of heroin, Red looked like he was dying of a dreadful disease.

"Ain't seen 'im like this before," Jimmie whispered.

I squeezed the gear in my pocket. It was just a few rocks, but, all the same, it was drugs. Aware of the predicament I was standing in, I toyed with the idea of bailing out, but decided that leaving would only draw unwanted attention to me. We watched the line of prisoners shorten until there was only Red left. The few granules the police had confiscated were just enough to enforce a petty possession charge. The fine was small, so we paid it and waited outside. There was no sign of Kira, but Jimmie insisted they must have released her or she would have been in the dock. Finally spotting Red, Jimmie whistled him over.

"You smell awful," Jimmie laughed, as Red arrived.

"I'll second that," I said, stepping back. "Here," I handed him the gear. "It's not much."

Already making for the tea shop across the road, Red was gone, making me and Jimmie shudder as he dodged the cars.

"Coffee it is, then." Jimmie grabbed my hand and used the other to hold up the busy traffic. We had just seated ourselves by the window when Red returned from the loos. Still ill, he moaned. So much so, that I gave him my last bit to shut him up. Jimmie broke all his rules and held up a newspaper so Red could snort. Five minutes later, sweat began retracting into the pores of his skin, producing a healthier pink glow, followed by a distant smile.

"What a fucking night!" Red said. "I'd just done a big one when the door caved in. Those bastards get bored too often for my liking."

"If you're gonna play with fire," Jimmie smirked, "you're gonna get your fingers burnt."

"Bradley, my man, long time no see." Jumping up, Red hugged the guy behind us. "Sit down. This is Sharm, and, well, you've met Jimmie, ain't ya?"

Bradley had short black hair and piggy eyes set in the pastiest of skin. "Yeah, the last big one, that was a good night if I remember right. You turned up with … let me think.

Fran, wasn't it? Nice girl."

Jimmie had the big smile I adored spreading across his face. Brad had dreadlocks flowing down his back, a dark tan, and plenty of chat. Though English, he had been born in Hong Kong. It took only a few minutes to realize how much he loved himself, not to mention his life. Having spent three months on business in Singapore, he was itching to let his hair down and celebrate his return home. An hour later we were sick of drinking soda and looking forward to the night ahead. Since he'd parked one of his dad's cars across the road, Brad offered to drop us back. I'd never been to Jimmie's side of town before and was surprised at how clean the area was. It made our end seem even grubbier. I watched Jimmie swagger away, his lean frame reminding me of a palm tree always. Brad then drove to our part of town.

"See you at seven," he said. "Grab a few others and we'll rock."

He was then gone, leaving a trail of fumes behind him.

Kira was back at Anna's. Like Jimmie said, the joint they'd confiscated from her wasn't worth the paperwork, so they'd detained her as punishment. The three of us smoked a joint together and refuelled our systems with heroin that Kira had scored. Red took his share and disappeared into the toilet.

Jimmie turned up early with Ness, followed five minutes later by Fran. It was good to see her; it had been a while. Waiting for Red, we played marbles, but the sound of them hitting the skirting boards must have been louder than we realised, hearing Anna approach we collected and put them away. Smiling predictably, Anna stood in the doorway; as she had nothing on us she put her hands together and backed away. Red appeared, dressed and was ready.

On time, Brad pulled up in his dad's sky-blue Jenson which wasn't big enough for everyone, so the others followed in a cab. The leather of the Jenson was fresh and soft. I sat sideways, stretching my legs out to avoid cramp. Red and Brad had obviously spent time together as they didn't stop talking. The loudspeakers in the back made it impossible to socialise so, bored, I skinned-up and hummed to *Corvette* by Prince. Halfway across town, the conversation grew louder and the word cocaine could be heard repeatedly. Once through the tunnel the road snaked up and around the mountains. I wound the window down and watched the smoke escape and dissolve into the night. Lights from wealthy houses seemed to wink as we passed. A mile or so on, Brad put his foot down on the accelerator and spun the car into one of the smoother drives. As he pulled up beside an identical Jenson I got out and stroked the bonnet of the other car.

"Nice set," I whispered.

"Not bad, huh," Brad smirked, "Dad does like his collectibles. Only two in the city, they're worth a fortune." Giving me the thumbs up Red smiled. Brad laughed as he dug his key out and approached the house. He was just opening up when the others arrived. I heard Ness gasp, and turned round to see Jimmie laughing.

"They're only statues," I heard him say.

As I looked around I saw stone shadows dotted all over the place. Brad took us all into the lounge, where he introduced us to his brother Piers, who placed his cocktail shaker on the side and shook a few hands before offering them drinks. Jimmie's head went up and down like a nodding dog as the introductions were repeated. Next to Piers were a couple called Ned and Lisa. Lisa was very reserved and seemed to be more interested in polishing glasses than in socialising. Ned, who was a little more hospitable, cleared the table and handed Ness a set of skinning-up materials. For a moment I watched her put the puff to good use; I was trying to figure out how the rolling machine worked when I heard Kira laugh. Standing next to Red, she was examining a large print on the wall. She cupped her hand over Red's ear and whispered something to him. I wasn't close enough to get the joke, but it amused Red. I had just joined them when I heard Brad.

"It's art, you fart, you gotta appreciate the strokes and have a broad mind. C'mon, it'll make more sense after another drink."

I stepped forward to examine the framed mess before me. I could just make out a pair of legs that were attached to a distorted dancer. The pastel texture gave it rather an unusual finish. I re-joining the others, sipped whisky and watched a second set of headlights appear in the drive. Brad made his way to the door, turned and smiled at everyone. "You're gonna love the stuff this baby gets." He opened the door and let in a Chinese couple. Ming Tsang and her boyfriend Way Lang came in and joined us at the table. Opening her handbag, Ming Tsang removed the largest ball of cocaine I had ever seen. From one of the cabinets Piers took down a large pipe that made pulses pump and eyes bulge.

"Who wants to start the ball rolling?"

It was the first thing that Lisa had said all night. Red took the ball and began to tap at its sides, breaking off small nail-sized bits. While keeping his eyes on the cocaine, Brad continued to pour brandy for his guests.

"How come we're smoking it?" I asked Red.

"Brad'll tolerate anything but needles," he whispered in my ear. Baffled by his statement, I watched Kira puff the first pipe load. The bottle filled with smoke as she sucked. She kept going till it was empty and her lungs were full. Unable to speak she just went with the ride.

My first pull on the pipe was powerful. My lungs held the smoke till they exploded with sparks. I went up in a lift and came down hard. It was the ultimate greedy experience, no different from doing needles, and there was no stopping us. Once we had all felt the lift, the conversation completely died and our greed began to show.

The rock turned minutes into hours and people into zombies. The consumption of whisky and cigarettes was the only thing holding our nerves together. We were on a never-ending roller-coaster that was stopping for nothing and no one. The rock never seemed to get any smaller, and we couldn't have got any higher if we'd grown wings.

Everyone looked ill, frayed and frantic. Jimmie shook his head every few minutes as though checking that his brain was still inside it. Kira's fingers were bright yellow from the nicotine that she had constantly balanced between them all night. The first to give up and go was Ned. Like a wounded animal, he retreated quietly to the nearest bedroom, shortly followed by Lisa. Using the person next to them as pillows, the others began to fall like a deck of cards.

My insides had become home to a circuit of vomit that threatened me each time I moved. Had it surfaced, I think I'd have choked. The white rocks on the table were calling, but so was another world. I couldn't feel a thing as my nails penetrated my legs. Had I closed my eyes, I know I'd never have woken up. I could take no more cocaine, my brain was screaming for it, but my body was dead. Unable to sit still or take any more poison, I began to pace the room.

Red oozed perspiration, reminding me of something that had been dragged through a rainforest. His eyes were as big as saucers, nerves raw he couldn't hold his fingers still. As his eyes followed me his head rolled back and forth. Reaching for me he pulled me toward him and spoke for the first time in hours.

"Do the brown if you wanna come down."

His eyes darted about the room, bouncing from wall to

wall and back again. I knew he was thinking about the broken rocks on the table. His greed was disgusting. Even though his lips were purple and his tongue white, he continued to gather pieces and burn the pipe just for the hell of it, not content to smoke alone he offered it to Kira each time too.

Hands unstable, I spilled more heroin than I was able to crush. Jimmie tried to help, but his hands were as fucked up as mine. Between us we couldn't have held anything still. I tilted my head and snorted the mess we'd managed to make on the table. As the hailstones tore and ripped at my nose, it began to bleed. I chewed my bottom lip and felt blood dribble onto my chin.

It was Kira who forced my mind elsewhere, beckoning me with her hands she looked only one step away from death. Foam had gathered around her mouth, eyes floating away she couldn't move properly. It was as if her whole body had become numb and now rusted. I crawled over to her and pushed the others away, she whispered stuff I didn't understand. I pinched her hand but the response was non-existent. Jimmie joined me, grabbed her other hand and told me not to let her sleep, that she had to stay awake. I shouted at the others to do something but their reactions were slow and instead of helping, Ming Tsang and her boyfriend made a quick exit.

"Cowards...!" Jimmie called after them, "no-good pie-faces."

Kira began to drift dangerously away. I took what little

water was on the table and threw it over her face. It worked, but within minutes she was slipping away again. As her eyes glazed over, her hand tightened around mine. I grabbed Piers, who was closest to me and shook him.

"Get an ambulance!"

He gazed at Brad like an idiot, then the swirls in the carpet.

"Useless cunt…!" Ness screamed at Piers, "we can't fucking well carry her!"

"By the time anything gets up ere it'll be too late anyway." Piers finally retaliated.

Brad got up and staggered across the room, instead of picking up the phone, he threw a bottle of smelling salts my way. He was being a prize prick, but Kira was more important than arguing with him. While Jimmie fetched bottles water, I waved the smelling salts under her nose. Verbal abuse jumped from person to person like fleas. The arguing did my head in, but combined with the smell it helped Kira from slipping away altogether.

Walk on the Wild Side

By morning we were no more than frail zombies whose energies had rusted to zero movement. I watched Fran exterminate her fag. It hissed like a snake as she buried it in the growing mound of stinking butts. Still damp from all the water, none of us was really comfortable. Kira shivered abruptly, but her smile was stable, if faint. Fran dealt some cards and played by herself to pass irritable time. I could hear Brad making tea in the kitchen, but my insides weren't up to it. As though she agreed about not wanting the tea, Kira looked at me and shook her head.

The table was a giant *Monopoly* board, only all the pieces were of higher stakes than the usual ones. It was the first time we'd had any cocaine left over after a session. Tobacco, papers, pipe cable, and dirty ashtrays swamped the wooden surface in front of me.

My eyes fell upon the centrepiece, on its side and burned black, the pipe looked as abused as I felt.

Still watching me, Kira pulled a yucky face and tightened the blanket around her. I walked outside to where Piers was sitting on a bench near the Jensons, he turned to me.

"The cabs are coming."

I didn't answer him. There was a few minutes silence before he attempted to break it.

"She had us all going for a while, didn't she?"

"Wasn't very nice, was it? Look, if you don't mind, I just want to be on my own."

I strolled into the garden, where, halfway down, I could hear the sound of birds. At the bottom was a large aviary, inside it exotic birds sat on bamboo poles while waiting for something to happen. Their eyes were sad, and I related to them straight away. Freedom was priceless, and the entrapment of drugs was no different from the prison of the cage. I never understood why people kept birds caged. If they were meant for enclosures, they wouldn't have wings would they?

I didn't hear Red, startling both me and the birds, he jumped out on us. Normally it would have been funny, but it wasn't.

"Cab's here."

His cheekbones protruded horribly from his face. The skin surrounding them sank like one of those cheap plastic dolls manufactured in China. Still coming down from the coke and feeling paranoid, I had nothing to say. As we walked back up the garden, his forefinger in particular seemed to twitch. We could see that the first cab was already occupied. Kira relaxed on the back seat using Ness to cushion her head while Fran sat up front.

I turned round to hear Brad making suggestions to Red.

"You wanna get away for a bit, it's not like you don't know anywhere, is it?"

Red nodded, but seemed to have his mind on other things.

"I don't ever want to do coke again," Brad tried to sound convincing.

I knew it was nothing but cheap chat and felt relieved to see the second cab arrive. Red patted his pocket and shook hands with Brad, a subtle nod and he opened the cab door. The leather seating was cold and the air-con made me shiver. Jimmie wrapped his coat round my shoulders and lit a fag. After two puffs, he handed it to me.

The ocean seemed to follow us part of the way back. Creeping round the rocks, the frothy white surf looked like a bubble bath washing the sand. I was grateful to nature for sparing my life and reminding me that there was more beyond the city I'd unintentionally chained myself to. I told myself I was giving it all up, starting afresh, moving out, and leaving the club. But, as the city below emerged, so did all its temptations.

I could smell the sea, ships, and boats. Fishermen didn't just fish. Some brought mountains of heroin from the mainland, and the energy fields that kept it all going tugged at my soul from every angle. As we stopped outside Anna's, Jimmie insisted on getting out and walking saying the walk home would do him good.

As I watched his long legs begin to strut along the street, I wondered where he got his energy from. On her way out Fran held the door open for me and Red.

"She just needs rest now, I've gotta get home." I turned to face Fran while I pressed for the lift.

"You and I both…"

"You don't really expect the lift to work, do you?" Fran sighed.

"It would be nice."

"Lots of things would be nice…" She trailed off.

Following Red I took the stairs.

"One day, Anna might fix something." I shouted down at her.

"You're having a laugh she's so tight she gave up smoking!"

"She had one with me the other day," I said, as I reached the top of the stairs.

"Exactly…" Waving a loose hand in the air Fran left.

Red went straight to the bathroom in my room. I knew he was hitting himself up, but was past caring or pretending I didn't know how deep his addictions were. He woke me some hours later with the smell of bacon.

"Thought you might be hungry now that the holocaust is over, Kira's okay. Just gave her a burger to bring her up. You know, I really think we should all chip off – to say, Manila for a bit."

I gave him a shifty look and began to eat. I knew my

skinny body wouldn't function on powder alone, though the thought of it was sometimes quite appealing. I didn't answer Red, I just ate. Screwing the takeaway paper into a ball, I got up and grabbed a towel.

"I'm going down the hall for a mo. Speak when I get back."

"What's wrong with this shower?"

"Nothing, I just fancy the other one."

I pushed Kira's door back, and looked in on her. The wrappers were still in her hand. She had eaten, but had gone back to sleep, so I left her. The smell of soap and musty water drifted around the shower room. I avoided the dead cockroaches and spun the handle. Stepping in, I let the water soak me. Thoughts floated around my numb nut like rice in a sieve. In a state of unfamiliar meditation, I stood there till the water went cold. I was shivering and jittery as I made my way back down the hall, using my coat as a dressing gown. I sat on my bed and tried to skin-up. Seeing me struggle, Red took the papers and began to roll for me.

"Come on, what d'ya think, we need a break. We'll all go, me, you, and Kira."

All I knew was that I didn't want to end up like Kira.

"Just another city, ain't it?"

"You gotta go there to get to the islands. It's pure paradise. Don't worry about gear, we'll take some with us, get off it slowly; clean ourselves up."

Seeming to doubt his own words, he paused. I didn't

answer, just drew hard on the joint he'd lit. The fear of having no gear was already taunting me, and we hadn't gone anywhere. I desperately wanted to be clean of heroin, but had become complacent with the lifestyle. Heroin cured all my problems, thoughts, and feelings. Life would be pretty painful without it. It was something I just couldn't imagine, so I didn't. Red didn't let up; every few minutes he would put up a good reason to go.

"What's worse, living 'ere with the rats or puffing in paradise?"

"Paradise sounds good."

It was Kira. She came in and joined me on the bed. Putting her arm round me she pulled me closer.

"Thanks for the other day, you're a star."

"I don't know how you kept it up, had us all going there you know. I mean, the stuff was oozing through your pores.

"Wasn't good, was it? And the dreams were just awful."

"That's why we need a change of scenery," Red interrupted. "Thai can get me a good deal at the moment, make things easier, won't it?"

"What, you want me to smuggle?" I said.

"Just a bit of personal, I'll take the rest. We can turn two grand into four if I get this right, then it's feet up, for as long as you like."

I twiddled my fingers while digesting the reality of his suggestion.

"And you have the funds for all this, do you?"

"No, but I got this." He held up a bundle of used news, "Brad wanted me to pick it up for him, decided I didn't like his attitude, so I'm borrowing it."

Seeking approval for his stolen contribution, Red threw the bundle onto the bed. Kira started to count the money, and heroin began to whisper.

I was seriously messed up. Doing gear on the beach sounded better than anything going on in the city. As Kira laid the last note down, she caught my eye.

"Three grand…!"

I hadn't told anyone about the account I'd opened to save for a down-payment on an apartment. I rummaged around, and eventually found the savings book that I'd stashed away. I had enough and more to match Red's steal, and, with Kira's contribution, we would be okay for a bit. I threw the book at Red. When he saw the sums, his eyes shone with satisfaction.

"More than enough, if you can get it sorted at your end, I'll do mine. And, if you're feeling up to it, Kira, you could go check out some flights."

The bank wasn't far; we went together and I gave Red what he wanted before making my second stop. Clubs were two a penny in Hong Kong, but 'City' was the best, not only did it pay the most, but was the safest. At first, Sassy was furious that I wanted out at such short notice, but when she'd run out of stuff to say she softened.

"I know about the drugs."

"You do?"

"I wasn't born yesterday the gloves, the moods, the bad timekeeping." She waved her hands in the air and smiled. "Come back good, huh?"

I watched her trundle off.

"That's the idea," I trailed after her.

I remembered that I kept a bit of cash in my locker so went and emptied it. It was only a hundred dollars or so but it all added up. It was while I was filling my pockets that I gave the place a final glance. Several faces I thought I knew nodded to me as I left, so many Asian girls came and went, it was hard to remember them all. The only permanent fixture seemed to be the Canton Queen, Honey, who was busy teasing the bouncers as I left, so I didn't bother her.

Back at Anna's, Kira had returned with the tickets and was busy throwing her excess clothes and designer labels into one of the hall cupboards. Sorting through my own, I too put them inside. Anna wasn't stupid; she never did anything for nothing and if we didn't return I knew she'd sell the lot. Anna waited for us to finish before marching down the hallway to collect her rent from some new travellers who were trying to knock her. Sharing a fag, we could hear her banging and shouting, the travellers ignored her until she put a key in the lock. The silence that followed indicated that they had paid up.

When she had stubbed out the fag, Kira told me in more detail about how she'd felt the night before. I listened with great sympathy and interest as she explained what she could.

She had wanted to stop but couldn't, until finally the poison consumed her. It was hard for her to explain the dizziness and tunnels – all she really remembered was drifting far away without any control. Finally, she changed the subject away from the drugs and told me about the time she'd dropped a whole crate of San Miguel, hearing the broken bottles, Pang had rushed in and done a war dance on the spot, making her and Fran laugh their heads off. It was good to see her smile and I told her about Harry, Claudia and Honey. We were still laughing when Red burst through the doors. White as a ghost, he threw a bag of heroin on the bed.

"It's pretty nerve-racking walking through the city with that much shit on ya."

"S'pose it would be," I said, stunned by the mass of heroin peeking through plastic bags. There was a lot, but it kind of made me feel safe, and the thought of cold turkey faded fast. I was glad there was no coke as it was expensive, crazy stuff. As she examined the heroin, Kira asked if he had got anything to smoke. Red dug in his side pockets and smiled...

"Always a bonus ball, baby," he said tossing her a ball of hashish before sitting down beside it.

"Looks like a lot of skinning-up's in order, aye. So, how's it all getting there?"

Cocking her head, Kira spoke in a sarky tone.

"You two take the personal. I'll have to put the rest up my arse, won't I?"

I detected resentment in his voice, or maybe she'd just

humiliated his male ego. Either way, cheap laughter lifted the atmosphere, making it all seem quite normal.

"Did ya get the tickets?" Red asked.

Kira opened the drawer and fanned herself with them.

"Nine-thirty tomorrow..."

"Good. Can't hang around with all this, we're cutting the edge staying 'ere as it is. I won't sleep tonight."

But that was run of the mill, because none of us slept. Every door sounded like a bomb, and every footstep seemed to stop right outside the door. Tossing and turning, I slept only briefly. Red was first up from the broken sleep pattern, and in the bathroom like a shot. I heard the tap run followed by the clicking of a lighter, a few seconds later the word "fuck" was flung out.

"He's burned his fingers," Kira said. "Either that or something else is up!"

Hearing Red moan we both let rip.

"Any one would think you were making a porno in there."

A red face appeared from behind the door and he curled his lip.

"I see you're back on form Kira."

"Now you know what it's like to be gay. You could make a fortune downtown."

"Yeah, about time you started selling your own sexy shit," I added.

He came out, a wave of embarrassment passing over his face.

"Bitches," he joked.

He had to laugh, or I think he would have cried. He handed me my share of the shit, and practised walking straight. My nerves drowned any further amusement I might have felt, and I became shaky. It was as though my nervous system had been plugged into an adrenaline socket, tense and twitchy they pranced and danced inside my skin. Seeing how bad they were, Red offered me a small pill pot and nodded.

"Take one. You'll forget you ever knew what nerves were."

Red had a cure for everything. Two Valium tabs later and I had changed from nervous wreck to frighteningly fearless. With nothing to do but wait, Red chain-smoked in subdued silence, whilst Kira farted around checking shit she had already checked.

The passports and tickets lay on the bed. Opening my own, I chuckled at my photo; I put it down and flicked through Red's. The comparison between him and his photo surprised me.

"Don't you look different?"

His cheeks were fuller, his eyes sparkling.

"Back home," he replied, taking the passport from me.

"What, did you just get itchy feet one day, and do the off?"

Ignoring the subject of family, he closed the passport and shook it in the air.

"These are big business out here, especially the diplomatic

ones. You don't expect people in authority to play the field, or carry stuff they shouldn't, do ya?"

"Depends what field ya mean. They use the club regularly. They're all big businessmen, but I don't think I'd want to nick their passports, not even for you, Red."

"Shame, we could make a mint."

Composing myself for a walk on the wild side, I didn't answer him.

The ride to the airport seemed to go on forever, and the plane was bang on time, which left me no time to change my mind. I sat quietly during the flight, dismissing horrible thoughts. But, as Red had promised, Customs was a piece of cake. They weren't the least bit interested in us, or anyone else for that matter. No longer walking the plank, we were free in the sun, unlike the residents of Manila.

Outside the airport, a wire barrier separated us from the poverty behind it. Fingers wiggled through the fence and desperate faces filled the gaps as they were squashed against it. There were women and children pleading for money and food anything they could make use of. Red tugged my arm as the cab queue shortened.

"Don't get sucked in."

"They're just kids!" I said, surprised at his comment.

"Yeah, smart ones at that," he went on.

"How can you be so cold?"

"What, d'ya wanna give all the money away on arrival?"

"No, but it ain't their fault if they're hungry!"

"Ain't mine either…"

"You got as much good in you as the sewers do clean water."

"Can we discuss this later?" Kira intervened.

Kira opened the cab door and threw her rucksack inside. Consumed with fear and adrenaline, none of us spoke as we were whisked into town. Turning off the road and down a beaten track, two stone lions that had ivy for hair decorated the entrance. Clumped either side of the drive daffodils danced in the breeze. Moving over the bumps we headed towards a stone building. As the old cab pulled up, a Filipina girl greeted us. After giving Red a hug, she showed us to a couple of adjoining rooms. They were bare and basic, but fresh sheets and water were all I wanted.

As she left, Red disappeared under the arch and Kira took to the bathroom. I threw my gear on the bed and myself after it. I turned on my side and began to empty my rucksack. When I had found my cigarettes, I stared at the ceiling and smoked. Pulling hard I tried to count the lumps of plaster out of which someone had tried to make patterns in. I think I got to thirty when a bad version of '*Lucky Star*' reached my ears. Kira often sang, but never so badly. Putting it down to nerves, I got up to shower. That was when I noticed something bulky stashed with my clothes and shit. I knew straight away it wasn't what I'd agreed to and blew a fuse.

"Where the fuck are you Red, and what about this?"

Storming through the arch with the package, I called again.

He appeared from behind the bathroom door, pain clearly displayed across his face.

"How could you?"

"Not now, can't you see how bad I'm suffering."

"Wos, it's stuck?"

"And it fucking well hurts..."

"Shouldn't be so greedy, should ya?"

"Well, I ain't sticking *my* hand up there." Kira stood dripping in the doorway quickly clicking onto his misfortune. Whether Red joined in out of anger or amusement I don't know, but it got his stomach muscles working, and five minutes later, he gave birth to twin hash balls.

"I'm sorry you picked the wrong bag up, Sharm, but what you don't know don't 'urt ya, right? I couldn't carry any more or I would have, wouldn't I? C'mon, there's twice as much to sell now. 'Ere, have a glass of this and think of the money."

"But it was okay for me, you selfish wanker." Kira laid one on him, slapping him hard. Red looked rather stupid with her handprint across his face, but he accepted it. He turned and opened a bottle of champagne.

"Oh, and by the way, I gave the maid a big tip for delivering this."

I didn't answer him and neither did Kira; we just both glared at him in silence. He poured the champagne out for us then began to cut up some of the hash.

"Please chill, don't be mad, we're here now, ain't we?"

"It's not the fucking point, is it?" Kira retaliated.

"Point is we got away with it." He waved the unlit joint towards me and then Kira. "Come on, try this."

"You're still an asshole," Kira huffed, taking the joint from him.

I hadn't had champagne for ages and began to feel dizzy. As I sank into the mattress, I imagined myself back on Harry's yacht. My dad was there this time, rambling on about money and where it was coming from. Tired of listening, I dragged myself into consciousness and wandered into the gardens. The fresh air tasted good. I heard the others before I closed in on them.

"You should have fucking well said something," I heard Kira say.

"I'm sorry, okay."

"Well, it just ain't good enough."

"There ain't nothing I can do about it now, is there?" Red finished.

Leaving them to their debate, I hung back. The peace was priceless, and for a moment took precedence over everything until my stomach decided otherwise. Desperate to avoid the perfectly pruned gardens, I began to run, but my legs failed me. I didn't make it back, and yakked all over the petunias. Luckily, it was only recycled beverage, so the mess was easily absorbed. It was some hours later that Red woke me and suggested we hit the town.

Manila was a wacky and wild place where women rode hard for a few dollars and men proved that they were nothing but monsters with mean appetites. I'd never seen such savagery. The guys were like rabid dogs, reaching and ripping at the girls as they served beer swill.

"Is this a funky town or what?" Red clapped.

I shot him a foul look.

"Don't you mean fucked up?"

"Yeah, Red," chimed in Kira, "what happened to women's lib?"

"If there were rules, people wouldn't be starving, would they, Kira?"

Before she could reply our presence began to cause quite a stir amongst the olive-skinned women. Seeing my camera, they rushed to the front of the stage where they had been dancing and began to pose. They thought we were reporters come to take photos of them and write about them, anything, that would save their souls from their present state of affairs.

"What now, Einstein?" I asked Red.

"Go take some pictures, it'll be fun."

"For who, them or you…?" Kira asked.

"Go on, I'll get the drinks in."

We moved closer to the stage, and took a few shots, but the girls were more interested in what we were wearing. They fiddled with everything from our belts to our earrings. One of the girls was so keen on Kira's beads that she let her have them. Another untied my hair bow and asked if she could wear it. I was just obliging when the grumpy little club owner came over and shooed them all back to work. I took the bow from my hair and threw it to the girl. Back on stage, I watched as the high heels caused blisters and burns. Some even bled. It was a mean deal – no dance, no dollar. *"Don't You Want Me, Baby?"* blasted its way out of the speakers and the girls went wild, making the most of every lyric and punter in the pad. I turned to Kira.

"Seems the only education needed is how to fuck a foreigner."

"Sure is!" a German answered, slapping my ass as he passed.

Having seen enough, we went outside and made our way to a place Red could only describe as Pig Square. It was a small place, again made up of foreign faces. As we got closer, we could see a mixture of folks roasting meat and swilling Spanish beer.

"This is more like it."

Red punched the air with a fist and whistled. The mixture of faces began to smile and cheer us into the square. I felt like a distant relative they hadn't seen for years, and just smiled at everyone. Holding up a skewer of uncooked meat, one of the Germans stepped forward to greet us.

"See you got yourself some good-looking couriers."

"Fucking cheek," Kira snapped.

"Didn't get shot then?" another enquired.

Red waved the comment away and got us a beer. With so many introductions happening at once, I couldn't remember even their first names, so I just nodded to them all. The smell of food brought my appetite to life, so, while the conversations churned, I ate well and tried to avoid the inquisitive questions that kept coming around. They wanted to know everything, but not everything was suitable to tell. Deceit and danger had drained me, and I was grateful for the flowing beer.

I don't know what time we headed back, only that I woke around midday to the sound of flies that were making the most of everything, including people. While I sank a whole bottle of water, my thoughts returned to the night before. I woke Red up and asked if what they had said about getting shot was true. Getting up, he was real grouchy.

"Yes, it's true! But I knew we'd sail. I've done this trip several times before. Is cool – we'll be out of here today."

"You pig."

I gathered the gear and stuffed it into one bag – my bag. I tore outside and sat on the bench, from where I could hear Kira bollock him, which didn't make me feel any better. I wanted out. Anywhere I could get peacefully tanked up with powder away from pricks and parasites. As an addict, I was grateful my gravy train wasn't about to dry up. As a person, the thought of someone blasting my brains out at point-blank range scared the shit out of me. Fact was I hadn't got caught. No one had blown my brains out, and I was still heavily addicted to drugs. Going back to Hong Kong with a bag full of gear wasn't an option, so when Red produced three tickets he had purchased from a pilot the night before, we headed off.

A bright yellow bus with noisy bells drove us out of the city to an old airstrip. The retired aircraft dotted around the field made the place look more like a museum than anything else. The broken wing of a Spitfire made a perfect place from which to escape the strong sun. Exhausted, we had little to say, so we sat quietly and watched some other travellers turn up and join the waiting game. As time rolled on, the sun became blistering and everything began to fry. Kira's makeup had melted slightly, and Red's cheeks burned like hot coals. Seeing our water disappear I spoke for the first time to Red.

"How long will it be?"

"Don't know. They don't rush here for no one – depends what state the pilot's in."

"Is that supposed to be funny?"

"Not really, got ya talking though, didn't it?" He opened the last bottle of water and swung it in the air, but Kira caught his arm and relieved him of it.

"You're such a joker at times. If the plane don't come soon, we're gonna shrivel up."

She drank half and handed the bottle back over. Twenty minutes later, we heard a faint buzzing, and a small dot appeared on the horizon, growing in size as it neared.

The pilot stank of stale beer, as he waved us onto the aircraft. Too lazy to get up, he took our money and tickets as we all boarded. The seat belts were broken, not that they would have made much difference. Once we were all on, the pilot fired her up and began chasing heat waves.

We flew low over sea and forest. At one point, we decapitated a tree. I raised my hands and looked at Red.

"Don't worry," he smiled, "you're in the Philippines now. It's all perfectly normal you know."

Poison Paradise

We hit the ground hard, skimming the earth several times before abruptly halting inside a strip of jungle. The sound of humming penetrated my ears. It was as though every lizard was singing at once. Stepping down the small ramp, I fanned myself with an old magazine I'd been reading and tied a scarf around my head. Red chucked his rucksack out. Following it he began to be stupid. Running towards the woods doing a poor impression of Tarzan I thought he looked a bit of a twat. The sound of engines diverting my attention, they roared through the trees, passed Red, and skidded before the plane where the drivers demanded $20 bills for transportation. Running back Red jumped on one of the bikes. As we entered the woods, the drivers began racing through the tangled trees. I clung to Kira's waist, turned and looked back. Our driver had taken the lead, temporarily losing Red and the others.

Five minutes later, we were standing on one of the world's most beautiful beaches. A silver almost magical mist covered the water, making the shells beneath look like pieces of ivory.

Heat ripples chased exotic fish through the ocean, their red and blue bodies beautiful against the shells. Half a mile out, golden sand framed the island in front of us. We must have stood there for a good ten minutes before the second bike pulled up. Red got off and joined us.

"What d'ya think…?" he enquired, dropping his bag.

"It's beautiful."

"Told ya you'd love it."

Red waved his arms in the air attracting the attention of a man in a small canoe-type boat approaching the shores. Since he didn't know that Red had been there before, the owner quoted us three times the price of a normal crossing. After a long haggle we were on our way, watching intently as the island grew closer and larger. Unable to resist the sand drifts, Kira rolled over the edge of the boat and stood up. Within minutes we were all waist-high, pushing the boat ashore. The owner got out and flumped on the sand where he waited in the hope of a passenger to take back.

We felt beckoned by the beach huts. Their bamboo windows made weird shapes, and their long stilt-like legs gave them individual, life-like characters. As we passed the huts I half expected them to start running after us. Wanting a set-back location, we took a smaller cabin near the trees. The owner, who was sitting nearby, wasted no time in exchanging the key for dollars. Inside, bamboo chairs and beds stood on similar legs to those of the huts. As we unpacked all the gear, the action made me take a step back.

"Eat your heart out." I felt Kira's chin on my shoulder as she peered over it.

"Looks like cold turkeys out the window," I said, crushing up.

"Umm, doesn't it just?" Kira knelt down and snorted hard.

Red was so busy making a fix, I don't think he heard a word either of us had said. I was glad I didn't inject; watching him made me feel queasy, it was foul. He joined us afterwards, and slurred his words.

"Thiss place heaaves at night, its quiiet naaw 'cos they're all sleeeping."

"Who…?" I asked him.

"Peeople. Travelllerrrs – you'll seee."

He went back inside and fell asleep. We watched the waves and listened to the birds until the sun set in all its glory. Somewhat hungry now, we woke Red and took our first wander together. The sand was still hot in places. Desperate to cool my bare feet, I found myself racing Kira in and out of the sea. I chased her through the waves, spraying the surf up as I went. Red caught up, and called our attention to a rock in the water.

"Watch out," he warned, pointing to it.

"For what…?" I asked.

"The lion-fish..."

He waded in and showed us one trying to camouflage itself in the sand. It looked harmless enough with its funny fat fins and fluttery eyes, but Red assured us that, if it stung us, we'd be in big trouble. He prodded it with a stick, pushing it back out to sea.

"They hide in the sand too, and there ain't much first aid in the hut, so take it easy."

Further along the beach, we came across a stack of logs and some leggy foreigners.

"Tonight you come, aye?" Two Swedes pulled out a huge trunk, threw it down and began to break it up. "We make fire and food tonight, if you want."

We shrugged our maybes and continued on our way.

"Like that all over," Red said.

I glanced back as I heard the wood crack.

"No shortage of party-goers then...?" I frowned.

"This island is one big party."

Red cupped my shoulder and steered me left onto a track. The shade enabled us to slow down and follow the shrubs. A small hut that sat between two palm trees in one of the clearings contained rows of cigarettes and sun creams. Behind the wooden counter there was a variety of canned drinks and crisps; pondering over the goodies, I rested my head on Kira's shoulder.

"Rothmans or Camels?" she asked, picking both up.

"I can't stand either."

"It's all you'll get here," a rough voice said.

I was more taken by the dreadlocks than the rest of the character trekking towards us. They twirled down his back and right round his chest.

"Kayden my man…!" Red was excited.

"Looking for good grub, right, Red?"

"You got it."

"Then you need to step this way. Old Mallie has a special tonight, served by some sexy help she's hired; not that you need any. So, you gonna introduce us or what?"

"Sharm, Kayden. Kayden, Kira."

"Very nice too…" Kayden threw both arms to the left, and smiled in a welcome gesture. As we headed into dense woodland, we waffled about everything and nothing until the smell of fresh bread made us change the subject. A few yards away there were five bamboo tables and chairs. Straw umbrellas, paper napkins, and tablecloths converted the place perfectly. It was strange sat at a table set in the middle of the jungle, surrounded by trees and unusual plants.

"This is a huge improvement," Red told us. "You should have seen the place before. It used to be just a quick takeaway through those shutters." Red pointed towards a freshly painted window frame.

"You been away too long. So what you got planned?" Kayden sat back and raised his eyebrows.

"Not a lot. Just gonna be kicking back with the girls."

"Ah, here she is," Kayden said as an olive-skinned girl holding a blue pad approached.

"You want mango or banana?" She asked.

We began with the mango, which was so good we drank a further three rounds while the omelettes cooked. After we had eaten our fill, we switched to San Miguel and chilled. I took my hair down, leaned back and arched my neck.

"Roots need doing." It was Kayden.

Glancing up from a weird angle, I saw him about to tug on the ends of it.

"You'll look like me soon." Kayden took hold of his dreadlocks and swung them round.

"No one could look like you," Red teased.

Kayden put his hair down, and went quiet before he continued, "so, you got anything else with ya?"

We remained quiet for a moment. I wanted to stay forever, and forever seemed possible if Red held back on the gear. Instead, he gave Kayden a nod that silenced him and put a satisfied smile on his face. We took out some hash, did one at the table and chilled even more.

As night fell and the stars sneaked through, we took it in turns to each choose one from the alluring sky. Captivated by their brilliance, Kira chose one of the larger stars just above her head. Red chose a cluster that consumed much of the north. I settled for the moon, as it was the largest object above and would hopefully ensure my safety. Kayden said he'd already had them all, as though they were women or something like that. Feeling tired, we all headed back to the beach. I thought we were lost until the fire the Swedes had built lit our path. They were making merry as they danced around the fire and sprayed each other with beer gas. As they saw us approach, they insisted we have a beer with them. It was good fun for a while, but the beer they had sprayed over us began to feel cold, so we left for the cabin and crashed out together.

I awoke to the soaring sweat of withdrawal, and an abundance of sores that irritated me as much as the gecko perched above. Half open, Red's mouth reminded me of a giant flycatcher. It wasn't a pretty sight, so I closed it as I passed. Kira was foaming slightly at the mouth, but I knew it was only the heat this time round and left her to sleep it off. I had just snorted a line of heroin when a young boy of around seven or eight came by shouting. I shoved the gear away, and went onto the veranda where he held up a tray of freshly-baked pineapple fritters for my inspection.

"Senorita, you like?" His little voice pleaded.

"Excellent," Kira chirped, charging up behind me. "We'll have the lot. Isn't it great we don't have to hunt for food?"

"Yeah, brilliant..." I cracked up laughing.

"What's so funny?"

"The thought of you hunting..."

"You want or not?" The lad tapped the tray impatiently while searching the beach for another buyer.

"Yeah, the lot…"

Kira disappeared inside the cabin, taking the tray with her. Quoting me $20 the lad held his hand out. I was about to oblige when....

"I don't think so, sonny."

Red grabbed my hand, put the money away and gave him

$10.

"Cheeky little shit. They learn young ere." Remembering our previous row, Red put the money back in my palm. "He don't need much, you don't see any shopping centres, do you?"

It was the first sensible thing he'd said in ages.

We had just finished eating when a German approached.

"Heard you have something to share, my friend?"

He spoke with a confidence that confirmed he knew about the drugs. Kayden had only been gone a few hours, but had had no trouble in spreading gossip. At first Red insisted we only had some puff to spare, but, as the day progressed, the pressure for something stronger grew. All sorts of folk were enquiring and wanted to buy a piece of the action. Since Red loved money as much as his gear, he was unable to stop himself. Germans, Swedes, and Yanks crawled out of the forest in the hope of a high. Apparently there had been no gear on the island for quite some time. I felt sick while I watched Red serve up. Most of them only wanted a bit of draw to suck in the sun, but the hard stuff began to spread like a forest fire. For many it was a dabble for others a chance to rekindle the habits that they had worked so hard to shed. Now the word was out, there was little peace our end of the beach. I wanted to avoid Red's dodgy dealings so went for a long walk up the beach. I ventured further than we had the first night, and came across a bar on the sand called 'The White Sail'.

Hundreds of footprints were embedded in the sand where free spirits had expressed themselves the night before. Inside the bar, on his knees, was an old man. Looking up, he asked me to pass him the spanner. Wires attached to an old box they snaked across the floor.

"No music, no movement. No movement, no money!" He said, taking the spanner.

I held the wires together and watched him tighten them, and then the box.

Afterwards, he gave me a bottle of water and sat a while with me in the shade. When he'd finished his drink, the old boy took a spear from a box of netting and approached the sea. He waded in, watching the water with intense patience. A few minutes later he speared a large parrotfish and smiled proudly. He slammed it down on the bar, lit his barbecue and began to cook it. It didn't take long. He cut the fish and placed it on small sticks for eating.

"You like?" Grinning he handed me one.

It was delicious. I hadn't brought any money with me, so as a thank you, I helped collect some of the beer bottles littering the place. I heard Kira calling my name before I saw her. Bidding the old boy farewell, I headed off. She had been up at the other end of the beach and had found a floating bar that she wanted me to see. Ten minutes later, she was shouting in excitement.

"There it is!" She pointed to the raft floating on the water, poised and beautiful it was awesome. Crushing fruit and ice,

Filipinos busied themselves serving the sunbathers aboard as well as the passing swimmers who hung onto the sides to take a breather. We ran to the shoreline, and raced each other to the raft. Having competed for the regional swimming championships back home, she thrashed me.

I couldn't believe how many people were out. Faces seemed to smile from every angle. As I soon discovered, not everyone partied all night, and not everyone desired the pleasure/pain path I was walking. We rolled onto the floating wood, ordered a drink and soaked the sun for as long as we could bear it.

When we returned to the cabin, we found Red snoring, needle still in his arm he looked awful. Plucking the congealed mess from his skin, I removed it and threw it on the floor. Due to the state of his arms he never joined in much during the day, they weren't just scared they were butchered. I was dozing in the shade when Kayden approached. Hot and flustered, he explained that some of the anti-drug users were pissed off that their paradise had been poisoned. Apparently a German called Kitch was threatening to stop Red. Pissed at Kayden for telling everyone in the first place, I shot him an angry look before I woke Red, but like everything else he just shrugged it off. Pissed off with him panic set in. If the antis stole the gear there would be none for us and I somehow couldn't imagine life without it, couldn't image not having my smoke screen. But with every packer knowing our pad, we were sitting ducks in the middle of no-man's land. Unable to get through to Red, I left for the beach.

Kira tried to talk sense into him, but it just ended in a loud argument that I could hear from the shoreline. I returned to find Red shaking hands with a couple of Bulgarians who'd made a large purchase of heroin. The fresh dollars on the side were very nice, but weren't gonna stop me from being sick. Unable to make head or tail of Red's actions, I poured gear in a bag and began to pack.

"What ya doing?" Red barked.

"Leaving… I've had enough!"

"We've only bin 'ere two weeks. Besides, you can't."

"Can't what?"

"Leave."

"What d'ya mean?" I was beginning to feel irritated.

"There's trouble in Manila."

"How do you know?"

"Fin the Italian returned earlier on the boat. He got out just as it was all kicking off, says they're looting and rioting in the streets. Besides, the airports have been shut down to stop Imelda leaving."

"Who the fuck is she when she's at 'ome?"

"President… She's been kicked out and the people want her blood."

Folding his arms, Red looked scared and smug all at once. While stuffing a bong, Kira's nostrils flared with anxiety. "How long before it's safe to go anywhere?" She managed…

"I don't know!" Red huffed.

Kira paused and struck a match. She dabbed the tobacco with it, and we smoked in silence. I didn't know how long I'd intended staying; you never know fuck all on heroin, your head's permanently up your arse. I did, however, sense a painful ride ahead. Kayden's arrival made no difference to the stale mood. On the contrary Red began to sharpen his only intravenous tool, twisting and twirling the needle along the side of his knife my teeth tingled. Exposing his butchered arms, he tried to hit up with a blunt needle. "Fuck this!"

Squirting the liquid from the needle into his mouth, Red then tossed it aside and stormed towards the jungle.

"Looks like the first aid hut's had it," Kayden said, chasing after him.

"Didn't know there was one?" I puffed.

"Yeah, heard 'em mention it the other day," Kira said. "It doesn't stock much, but there's bound to be one needle there."

"The guy's relentless!"

While I sorted and stashed some gear, Kira got the bong going. Stoned, I stared at a pile of ropes one corner of the cabin. I got up to put some music on and tied the ropes together. A hammock I raised it before Kira. "Time to put these up…"

Together, we went to find some suitable trees. Putting them up was one thing; getting in was another! The first one fell down with me in it, which caused great amusement. A

Filipino, fishing in the surf, watched as we tried again. I could see him laughing under the sun hat that covered his head and shoulders. He put his rods down and waded our way. "That's not how you do it, girls."

Taking the two ends, he found some notches in the trees near our hut and tied strange but strong knots together. We thanked him climbed in and swung softly for some hours.

I heard the lads before they were visible. As they passed us, they sounded a lot happier. When they reached the veranda, they prepared a hit in the spoon before sucking it up with the stolen needle. I knew Red would struggle to hit up, he always did. Examining the scratches, scars and torn skin on his inner arms, he tightened the belt with his teeth, spearing broken skin he missed. On his third try, blood ran down his bulging arms.

"Why don't you just bloody well snort it?" I cried in disgust.

"It's not the same, Sharm." His teeth were gritted.

When he pulled the needle back a fourth time it filled with blood, releasing the belt he fell back. I turned away from him to see one of the island's stray dogs and called to it. Its eyes were friendly as it approached.

"Tell it to go," Red slurred, "it's only on the scrounge..."

"Oh, shut up, Red," Kira snapped, calling to the dog.

"If you start feeding them," Red continued, "we'll have every stray dog on the island round."

I laughed aloud. "Unlike you, Red, they have their good

points."

"Enlighten me." Sarcasm rippled as he sat up.

"They're loyal, and don't shit on you."

The smile left his face instantly. "Meaning…?"

"Whatever you want it to. Don't tell me you were one of those deprived kids back home, who never had a dog."

"What the fuck'r you on today, you got a period or wot?"

"Thanks to you, that's one problem I don't have!"

"Leave it out." Removing the used needle from his arm Kayden raised his head and slurred his speech. "We're meant to be mates."

"Whatever!" Getting up, I walked off. I don't know why I had the hump. Well, I did, but I didn't. Red rattled me and was getting on my nerves big time. I'd gone a hundred yards or so when I heard Red catch me up. In his left hand was my cotton scarf. He bent down, dipped it in the sea and handed it to me. It was cool on my head, but I struggled to tie it, so Red took over. For a moment he stood motionless, almost trapped in his own skin and shadow. And then, as if by magic, he snapped out of it.

"Come on, I know a great place to eat tonight."

"Just stop selling the gear. Ain't exactly what we planned, is it?"

"There ain't much left now anyhow."

"Exactly..."

We were about to move off when two figures carrying surfboards forced their way through the trees. I knew they were the German antis by the unwelcome frown they gave Red. Stopping the taller of the two asked if I was okay. I knew one wrong word was all they were searching for. I nodded and watched them move off, kicking the sand as they went. Red took a deep breath and spoke.

"The tall one's Kitch, the other's Runny." Red lit a cigarette. "You know they want my blood, don't ya?"

"I thought you knew everyone?"

"Nearly everyone…"

"How come you know their names?"

"Kayden. He sometimes surfs with 'em – well, he used to, anyhow."

"We best avoid them then, aye."

"That's what I've been doing."

I soaked my legs in the water. The small pimples the mosquitoes had left were turning into sores.

"You shouldn't scratch 'em," Red advised.

"Easier said than done, come on, race ya back."

I was surprised to see that the other two had tidied up and ready to go out. Taking one of the many back tracks, we began to walk through the woods. The clubhouse was set well over the other side of the island. We got a little lost, but the sound of 'Dire Straits' reeled us in. The place was nothing special, and with dusk falling it made no odds to me. While the lads went to see what was on offer, Kira handed me a cigarette.

"What d'ya see in that guy?" she giggled, "It's not like 'e's good in bed or anything, is it?"

"'Ow would you know?"

"Cos the only prick 'e's ever given you is in the arm."

Bursting into laughter, I choked on the smoke. Kira never said much, but was the bollox when she did. The sandwiches ordered by the lads had stringy stems hanging either side of them. I nibbled the edge of one, but the taste and texture put me off. I opened the bread, mushrooms inside I knew they were magic. Kira picked up what I'd put down and took a bite.

"Tastes bloody awful," she spat.

"You know something, you're right."

Red stood up and strolled back to the owner. A moment later, he returned with a pot of jam, stuffed the mushrooms inside and swilled it all around.

"Try them now," he said emptying the jar out. I poked at the slug-like texture and declined the offer. Kira dared herself to try another, but gave it up as a bad joke and took to the rum. Five minutes later, the lads had eaten the lot and joined her.

I saw a dog approach in advance of its owner.

"That's Jet," Kayden said, calling to it.

A few moments later we were joined by Fin the Italian. Being the only permanent resident on the island, he was well respected. Tall and slim, his string sandals and satchel made him every bit the Robinson Crusoe he was. Just back from Manila, he put his goods down and filled us in on the madness there. Apparently, the ghettos had gone into autopilot and people had stolen enough goods to start their own businesses.

"You should see the place," Fin said. "It's like a bombs hit it. There ain't a shop not been stripped of something, military are cleaning up now."

The conversation was cool until the mushrooms took effect. That's when Red and Kayden began to dance and sing the most awful songs. They entertained us for half an hour or so before they hit the deck and fell asleep. Fin pushed his shoulders back and his head forward.

"Stoned, on magic mushrooms," I said, "they'll be okay tomorrow."

Laughing, Fin put his fingers to his mouth and whistled to Jet. The dog bounded in and soaked Red's and Kayden's faces in saliva.

"He's probably hungry," Fin said. "Wanna walk?"

"Why not," I undid Red's money belt and took it before someone else did. "Nothing happening here now…!"

"Hang on, I've got an idea." Kira took a lipstick from her bag and began to paint. I stood back with Fin and watched her put big Vs over the boys' brows and give them both giant 'bottle lips'.

Fin fluffed Red's hair up and placed his arm over Kayden. "Now they look like a pair of proper girls."

"Wait, not quite…" I took the ribbon from my hair, put it round Red's forehead, and tied a big bow. Giggling, we headed into the woods. It was dark, but Fin knew the way well. To make the long walk easier, Fin told us about himself. He had been on the island for two years, during which time he'd purchased a piece of land and built on it. Allowing the previous owner free residency meant he always had someone to maintain the place. He'd also built a bar for himself with other ideas in mind, but they hadn't quite paid off. By the time we reached the last track, we were done for, so we slept till light arrived.

The cabin was basic – much like our place on the beach, but outside it was beautiful. Set in a circle of clear land and surrounded by trees, the place was quite secure. Two properly secured hammocks swung from side to side, near them stood a well-built bar. Bells hanging from the entrance they chimed, to my right was a smaller dwelling.

"That's the Filipina Paulo's place," Fin said, as he joined me. Paulo then appeared from inside the hut, fed the hens and hung two dripping shirts out to dry.

"I wonder if Red realises what he looks like," Kira said stepping down from the entrance.

"I'm sure he will manage to smile," Fin said, heading towards two large water butts. He checked they were full and fresh, dunked a bucket and walked towards the trees.

The simplicity of Fin's life was remarkable, and I couldn't help secretly yearning for a piece of it. Being away from the world was rather appealing – no people, no problems. Only I did have a problem – one I didn't know how to deal with.

Making my way over to the bar, I executed it in private with Kira. We opened a small bag of heroin and took out enough rocks to satisfy ourselves. Using a nearby stone, we crushed and snorted, wiped the wood clean of drug dust and went to find Fin. Stood knee high in the shrubbery he was watering something. The partially-shaded vegetation hid the plants, but not the smell of cannabis.

"It's my winter stock," Fin said, without turning. "When it rains it rains hard, sometimes for three months nonstop."

"Don't you get bored?" I asked, amazed that anyone would want to stay under such dismal circumstances.

"If I get bored, I go see my girl in Manila."

"What about the riots?"

"She has a place outside the city. Come."

He trekked over to the bar we'd come from, disappeared round the back, and returned with some stools. We sat down and began to skin- up some of his grass. I offered him some of our hash, but he refused, saying his was best. He sparked up, and went inside the bar. Removing a sheet of canvas, he revealed a fridge, generator and sound system. Above them on a shelf some glasses had gathered dust and some old boxes were piled high. The place just needed a good clean-up.

"It's a shame. This bar was to be my business, but I discovered people are too lazy to trek out here."

I hated to see something good go to waste.

"We've got nothing to do. Maybe we could jazz the place up a bit. Paint some signs and dot 'em along the tracks."

Kira nodded in agreement.

"Okay, let's give it a go. You can have half the cabin as payment if you like. It might save you and Red some money. Call it an exchange for trying to get the bar going."

Paulo a sun baked peasant approached from the trees, making me jump and Fin laugh. We watched as he carried cut logs back and forth. After he'd stacked some neatly outside Fin's, he made his own personal pile before resting in the sun.

"He's no bother," said Fin, "usually drinks himself to sleep after working. Listen, I need bread from Mallie's, so I can walk some of the way back with you if you want. Come back when you like."

Fin knew the walk like the back of his hand, but for us it was just a maze of shrubbery. I was surprised at just how many tracks there were snaking off in all directions. Seeing this we put branches and lumps of wood out as reminders. Kira and I split from Fin at the beach, and returned to the cabin.

Red was snoring like a pig, still covered in lipstick. Kayden wasn't with him, so I assumed he was walking round the island looking bright and bubbly. I slapped Red to wake him up.

"What's that for?"

"Mosquito," I lied, on seeing the handprint. "Come on, we're moving."

"Where…?"

"Inland," Kira said, scooping up some scattered

belongings. "We can't afford this much longer anyhow."

"Wot, Fin? I thought he was a loner."

"Well, he just expanded!" I said wrapping up what gear was left. Red rolled onto the floor and found himself face down. I thought he'd hurt himself, but instead he started to giggle. We had been so busy getting stoned that none of us had noticed just how much rock had fallen through the floor. I laughed with him as we crouched and peered through the floorboards. Below us lay a golden pancake covered in white sprinkles. We drew straws on who was to go down and begin the delicate job of collecting. Kira drew long, so we left her to pack while we picked. We had been down there only five minutes when we heard voices speaking with Swedish accents.

"There's nothing left," we heard Kira shout.

"How can there be nothing!"

The voices grew louder and harsher. Pissed off with Red, I raised my eyebrows.

"It's Muzz and Emelio," he said.

"Don't matter who it is, it needs sorting, don't it? These guys are sick and we're the only ones with anything."

Red called to the Swedes. "Down here, Muzzy. It's pick-your-own today."

A few seconds later, two flushed faces appeared. I watched the sand stick to their sweaty fingers as they grappled and snorted at what they could. By the time they left, they looked like sandpaper decorated with snow.

Sleepyheads

I felt relieved to get away from the beach. Following some of the landmarks we'd laid out it wasn't difficult to get back to Fin's. Jet was the first to meet us, then Fin who whistled from behind the bar. He opened beers and set them on the newly-polished bar top, stood back, folded his arms, and laughed at Red.

"They still haven't told you, have they?"

I knew straight away that Fin was on about Red's bottle lips and eyes. His lips had faded but the eyebrows were still visible.

"Told me what?"

Fin took his shaving mirror out and held it up for Red.

"Shit, man, and Kayden…?"

"Like a clown," I laughed.

"Fucking hell man," yelled Red, "I thought the weird looks from Muzz and Emelio was over the gear."

Dunking a scarf in the water butt, Red began to wipe his eyebrows.

"All good fun…" Fin walked towards the generator and patted it twice. "Once we get this baby rocking, everything will work. Saw Cameron earlier, he's doing some special baking. Oh, and I heard a ships been spotted round the north coast. If there's any supplies left on board we may be next."

Feeling excited, I rummaged for my wallet. No longer overflowed with dollars, it was thin, worn and frayed around the edges. I glanced at the others and could see the same thought had gone through all our minds, a quick getaway back to Hong Kong before the sickness set in. Kira wiggled her nose and frowned harder than ever.

"Nice idea, but it's better if we stay here now." It did seem more sensible to go sick in the sun than maybe get caught in hell halfway. Red's silence was a bad sign, it meant that his mind was conjuring up another shite plans. Maybe this time he was thinking of hijacking a ship to replenish all the islands as they ran dry. He could sell everything at treble the usual price and knew it. I could just see him haggling over water and tobacco with the locals. While I daydreamed, Fin was carefully cutting and placing some of his best gunga sticks onto a handkerchief. Once they were all side by side he folded everything into a neat bundle and tied it with some cord.

"No Paulo?" Kira asked, looking at the surrounding bushes.

"He's around." Fin blew smoke to his left. "Probably collecting mushrooms for his tea."

"Magic…?" Red perked up.

"Maybe," Fin smiled. "Maybe that's why he's so wacky

half the time. He knows exactly what's in these woods and where to find it."

Pointing to the faded lipstick on Red's eyes, Fin chuckled.

"Maybe leave the mushrooms a while huh, what happened to Kayden anyway?"

Red scratched his head, having to think. "Said something about playing ball, but then it could have been the falls."

"The falls…?" Intrigued, I wanted to know more.

"Yeah, they're about half a mile that way." Red swung round, pointing to his right. "Everyone goes there at least once, but the bikers are out of gas. If Kaydens gone it'll cost him."

Water sounded soothing; the sores on my legs were getting worse, they had deepened into small, crater-like holes. Fin, seeing the infected buttons running up both my legs, jumped over the bar and went into the cabin. Five minutes later he returned with a pair of cotton baggies.

"Here. If you can keep them on, it will help."

Fin was real tall and my short legs failed to fill the trousers, rolling them up to my ankles I turned the waist down.

"Not sexy anymore," Kira said.

Thank fuck for that, I thought, suddenly aware that she might actually fancy me. Fin found the comment quite amusing. Arms folded and half-leaning in the doorway, a funny little grin crossed his face.

"Well, unless there's anything else, I'm off to get a hash cake baked. Any donations would be greatly appreciated." Fin paused and turned to Red.

We'd known that it would be needed when the gear ran out, so we'd hung back on our draw, but even in our state knew it was rude not to oblige Fin. I'd never heard of hash cakes, but Red insisted they were good. Stuffing the gear Red had given him into the middle of his satchel, Fin wandered into the sun. He was so cool I doubt he ever felt the heat.

After we had checked out the cabin and sleeping arrangements, we went to see how the cannabis was doing. Having been watered, the healthier plants were poking their pointy leaves at the sun. Kira rubbed a sticky pod between two fingers.

"They smell real good!"

Red took the clump from her and put it in his mouth.

"We could always chew them if things get too bad."

"I'm sure Fin wouldn't thank us," I said, shooting him an angry glance.

"Yeah, yeah, I'm only joking, what about a stew or tea instead?"

"Right now, a line will do."

Kira headed back to the cabin and disappeared for a moment. When she returned, she made for the bar and emptied some gear out. With only a few days' supply left, the atmosphere was tensing up, especially since Red had snapped his needle and wanted a whole lot more heroin to satisfy his nose. As Kira pounded rocks beneath her knuckles, I watched as her veins strained like swollen rivers about to burst their banks. I think that's how we all felt, ready to explode. With the powder rowed up, she spun one of our only notes.

"Me, first," said Red.

"Says who?" Kira scowled. "You ain't in charge no more Red. Why should you always have more?"

"Because ..." Red hesitated. "Just hurry up will ya!"

Two seconds later one line was gone forever. With the note still up one nostril, Kira pressed the other and fired. Like a dart the note flew my way. I caught it and snorted while Red moaned about the wait. Desperate not to think of withdrawal, I got up to investigate some brushes which Fin had put into soak. Beside them was a piece of wood he had cut to make a sign that would direct drinkers our way. I opened the tin of paint and swirled the brush around; I'd just flicked the excess away when....

"You're taking the piss!" Kira shouted.

"Ain't my fault I need a bit more!"

"Ain't my fault you use a needle."

"Ain't mine either."

"You sold everything."

"In case you hadn't noticed, food costs money."

"Is that the best you can come up with, wanker?"

And so the rowing over gear had begun. Tearing strips off each other like a pair of piranhas, Red and Kira were doing my head in. The louder they got, the faster I painted.

"Why the fuck don't you just finish it all up!" I eventually screamed.

They stopped as they both turned to face me, but a moment later they were off again. Having written on the wood, I took it up the track wet. The top of the track was deserted as always, but I stood the sign in the sand just the same. Maybe some wanderers would see – maybe not. Either way I was glad to have escaped the atmosphere. I wanted to continue on to the beach, but had forgotten my hat and was already burning. Turning back, I stayed close to the shrubbery in the hope of protection. I knew the last bit of gear was doing all our heads in. Holding onto it was making us edgy and horrible. There was no reason to make it last. The crunch time was here and I just wanted to do the lot, get it done, let it all begin, shut everyone up and accept the pain that was coming. Pretty mad, huh, but that's what heroin does. It screws you up, makes you selfish, horrible, and totally insane for a while.

When I reached the clearing, I couldn't see Red, but leaning on the bar Kira was skinning- up for two military officers. I'd heard they occasionally passed through the islands to see what was going on. Relaxed their guns were laid on the bar. I didn't know what to do and hung back. While the military puffed on the joint, Kira examined the shooters. I searched the perimeter a second time for Red but he was gone. Had he pissed her off that much? My mind wandered.

Five minutes later, the officers stubbed out the joint. Taking their guns back, they walked back through the bushes and disappeared.

"Where's Red?" I asked making my way over to her. "And what did they want?"

"Red ran that way." She pointed to a well-trodden walkway. "Cops were just passing and fancied a bit of what they could smell, said they'd rather smoke it than take it away."

"But it ain't even ready."

"I know. I had to use our last bit to keep 'em sweet."

"This place gets crazier by the day." I blew out my cheeks.

Charging through the trees Red appeared. "Take it that it's safe to come out?" he enquired.

"Had to use our last bit of draw though," Kira sat down, sulking.

Red was twitching with temper, cold turkey fast creeping in another argument was on the way.

"Let's just get it out the way and finish everything!" I strolled to the hut.

"Make it a whopper," Kira shouted.

"No way…"

I could hear Red moaning, but I was way past giving a shit about anything he had to say. Searching for the last drabs of everything, I poured it together with my own secret stash, making the last lines huge. Instead of thanking me for the extra, Red moaned, just moaned his head off till the gear slowed him down. We dabbed the decking till there was nothing left. Afterwards we lay content in the shade, listening to the rhythm of the jungle hum and hiss. It was a strange silence, one that announced the end of a very long session, leaving nothing more to bitch about.

I awoke to the sound of jingling bottles and barking. I could see Fin trundling down the track, carrying a tray of food, accompanying him and treading carefully, was a stranger I hadn't seen before. Red got up and went to meet them; a moment later he stopped abruptly and rubbed his hair nervously. The German antis were behind Fin carrying a crate of beer. One had a guitar in his spare hand, the other some tools.

"Just wot I need today of all days!"

"We ain't got nothing left," I said joining Red. "And by the looks they're here to party. Besides, Fin must have said we were here."

Within minutes they were all round the bar calling for us to join them. I pulled up a stool, sat down and nodded to Fin, who eagerly introduced everyone.

"This is Cameron he bakes a mean cake man. I don't know if you've met Kitch," Fin turned, throwing his head at one of the anti's. Kitch had a gorgeous smile, but refused to share it with Red. Taking a spanner from Fin, Kitch turned his attention to the wires and cables on the floor.

"Come to get me generator working, I hope," Fin continued. "And this is Runny, always up for a party, no matter how small."

While Kitch worked on the generator, we helped Fin to

hang the rest of the lights he had in the store. Twenty minutes later the generator fired up; it was loud but the sound of Supertramp soon killed it. Exhibiting a hint of blue, the bulbs worked, which gave a whole new meaning to dusk.

"Now we're ready."

Cameron pushed his stool back. With a smile he brought out the freshly-baked hash cakes. Tufts of green poking out of the sides they looked weird. Fin was the first to taste them. With a look of satisfaction on his face, he told me to try one. I'd eaten very little all day and my passion for food was growing by the minute.

The first went down a treat. Taking a second I stopped and examined it, broke a cocktail stick in half and gave it arms.

"Hey, this looks like Kayden," I shrieked, "only he's shrunk!"

It was the first time Red had laughed properly since the arrival of the Germans.

"I don't know how the guy lives in this heat with so much hair," he said, taking one of the cakes.

"Where's he gone again?" Kira mumbled as she munched.

"He goes exploring sometimes," Red replied.

"If you want to explore, mine's the place."

We turned to face Cameron.

"Certainly is," Fin nodded, "right amongst the stars."

"Stars?"

"Can't leave without seeing these ones." Fin insisted.

Still starving I kept eating.

"Take it easy." Cameron winked, as Kira tried a third.

With the fridge now humming away, Runny began to fill it. "D'ya know how lucky we all were to get this lot? Ain't what ya know but who…"

"I'll drink to that," Kitch put the tools down and came up for air and a beer. "That should do you a while, my friend. Just remember which wires go where."

Taking a beer from Fin, he sat on the furthest stool and drank it. On my fourth cake, I began to giggle at nothing. By the fifth, the others appeared to be blurry – almost fuzzy at times, a bit like the folks as they get beamed up in *Star Trek* and disappear into millions of tiny particles for a few seconds. Everything had become quite amusing; in fact, the whole fucking world became a fuzzy joke. Kira joined in, and for a moment, our laughter drowned the music.

"Bloody 'ell, they've eaten the lot!" Fin yelled.

"They haven't, have they?" Cameron cut in. "They're gonna sleep for a week. I loaded them up good 'n' proper. An elephant could have got stoned on that lot."

"Were they good?" Red droned.

"Fabulous," Kira swayed. "How was it for you?"

Before he could answer, my imagination began to run riot. Grabbing Kira's arm, I began to laugh my head off.

"D'ya see wot I see?"

"Where…?"

"There," I pointed towards Red, "the dog in the suit."

He had become a pug standing on two hairy back legs. He wore a blue suit covered in buttons that were nearly as big as the finger he shook. Something about selfish cakes made me laugh even more. I laughed till my muscles felt bruised and my belly nearly burst. When I could laugh no more, a nasty sickness overtook me, and the urge to lie down became overwhelming.

I used Kira as a prop, and we staggered to the cabin, giggling at everything we could make out in the dark. We climbed the steps and I turned to look back at the lit bar. The lads were still there. Their arms moved about as the five of them raised beer to their mouths. After that, there was nothing but sleep for us.

I had become acclimatised to the temperatures, so knew it was around midday when I woke, I also knew I had withdrawal symptoms. In the beginning, I felt just like I had the night the police had raided Anna's – a mild form of flu and very miserable. But the heat made the sweat ooze from my pores and my own stench forced me up and out. The place was quiet. Cameron and the others had obviously left during the night. Outside, Red was on the wooden steps, unintentionally blocking my way. Stepping around him, I sat down.

"No Fin?"

"Gone to see what grub's about. Things are running low and in demand now …" He paused and lit a cigarette, pulling harder than ever on it, he got up. "It's on its way."

I didn't want to know what he meant, but I did.

Inside, we could hear Kira tossing and turning; a moment later, we heard her mumbling obscenities. As I wiped perspiration from my nose, I turned to Red.

"It's gonna be bad, ain't it?"

"Yep... It's a bastard! This time tomorrow you'll know all about it." He jumped up and paced towards the hammocks and back. "He's a fucking nutter out to get me!"

"Who…?"

"Kitch – who d'ya think?"

"He seemed okay to me."

"I don't see 'ow anything could have looked okay to you – your eyes were as glazed as fucking cherries when you crawled away from the bar."

"You're just being paranoid!"

My head was beginning to hurt like never before and I couldn't be bothered to listen to his self-pity. It wasn't my fault Kitch didn't like him, I wasn't even sure I did anymore. I knew Kira was up when a pair of shoes missed my head by a few inches. After them came a string of cups, hats and books. Fortunately, my beach bag and baggies also came through the door too. That's when I knew it was time to leave. With the shakes and bones that were beginning to feel like warm jelly, I pulled my sneakers onto my lumpy feet and headed for the beach, where I stayed for most of the afternoon. Slumped on the sand I let the water wash over my holey legs. The salt water was the only thing that helped my mosquito infections.

Getting sicker by the minute, my body felt like it was falling apart, like someone was undoing the invisible seems that kept it all sewn together. The scabs came off my thighs, leaving craters of raw flesh, ugly and sore I pulled the pants Fin had lent me over my ankles and up my legs. Hungry I made my way to the nearest beach hut, whose shelves held only half their normal quota of goods, I needed a fag, but most cigarettes were nearly out. I bought some dried beef and biscuits along with two packs of fags. I had just lit one when I saw Muzz and Emelio approach from the far right. I didn't really know them. The brief encounter at the beach hut had hardly been a social call. The long faces and fluttering hands told me they too were unwell.

"We've been back to your place sieving sand several times – but there's nothing left…"

Stealing the conversation, Emelio took over. "You ain't got nothing, 'ave ya, Sharm?"

I kicked sand over the front of my feet and shook my head offering them a fag was all I could.

"We're building a fire for tonight." Rubbing his skin Muzz spoke while lighting up..

"What for…?" I asked.

"Take our minds off the suffering, I suppose. His voice was full of irritation.

"Okay," I said, "where?"

"There's a clearing, few hundred yards past Mallie's; only place suitable if we're not to cause a forest fire, you'll see it once it's lit. Most folk will be there."

"Okay, I'll let the others know."

As I walked back, I felt an indescribable hunger come over me and I just had to eat. By the time I reached the top of Fin's, I'd consumed a whole packet of biscuits and some of the beef. As I neared the clearing, I saw Kira standing motionless in the middle of it all. She was making a stop signal with her hand so I obliged. A few seconds later I felt someone watching me, and it wasn't Red.

I turned slowly to see cave-like eyes staring at me from the woods. The man was near-on naked, so I knew he was a native. The dark figure didn't move, just observed me from between the trees where he stood. At first I was afraid, but quickly realized he meant no harm. As Red began to approach Kira, the native made off into the undergrowth.

"Wait!"

I put one foot into the shrubbery and paused, though sick, curiosity got the better of me. I threw my bag on the ground, shooed the others away and ran after him. I don't know where my strength came from, but I found myself jumping shrubs and the occasional log until a tiny clearing appeared. My native wasn't there, but two small kids around seven or eight were. They were sitting on a fallen trunk playing with leaves and mud. Nearby a woman collected mushrooms and berries that she skinned with her teeth. She was obviously unthreatened by me as she continued to skin the berries and hand them to her children. I crouched quietly, admiring their survival techniques; their acceptance of having nothing, they didn't know or need gadgets. They were resourceful and grateful for whatever came or grew their way. They didn't inject shit into their bodies and have to keep running from themselves. So who were the idiots here, the ones living off the land or the ones ruining it in the name of civilization, the ones who needed very little or those using the needles? The land made them strong, and I was honoured to have spent time with them, no matter how short. My temperature was again rising when I could hear the others catching up.

"Bloody 'ell!"

Shifting her weight Kira leaned on me.

"Aborigines," Red whispered, "quite rare to see them."

"Then I'm glad I did. They say the best things in life are free."

"Leave you 'ere then, shall we?"

"I wish!"

Knowing the moment was gone I got up and headed back.

"Wait up, Sharm, jus' joking," promised Red.

"Well, maybe I don't like your jokes anymore! When do you ever say anything funny, clever or intelligent? You got us into this shit and you do nothing but talk shit!"

"You're such a dick at times!" Passing him Kira caught me up.

"Did you get any food, Sharm?"

"A little..."

We came out of the woods, and I searched for my bag. I

saw it in the shrubbery, and we both began to run towards it.

"You're gonna share, ain't you?"

With one hand on his hip, Red reminded me of a Roman statue, only he had his clothes on and lacked the elegance of a centurion, certainly not something that would match the criteria if in a nude. I pulled dry beef from the packet and handed it out, while they devoured it, I told them about the fire. Red didn't answer, he just chewed.

"Can I open these?"

More interested in food, Kira tore at the biscuits and kept rummaging in the bag searching for more.

I knew the fire would be a long walk especially feeling half dead, so I left the possibility of going for everyone's digestion. With nothing left to do, I rolled into one of the hammocks and curled up. Only one other hammock spare, Red had to make do with an old inflatable bed that Fin had knocking about. We were an hour into the dead zone when our brains experienced unwanted pounding. I looked up to see Paulo swinging a hammer above his head.

"He would show up now, wouldn't he?" Kira stuck her fingers in her ears.

"Unfortunately, he lives 'ere," I said.

"Hopefully he'll go away again!" Unwilling to get up, Red covered his head with a pillow.

"Ya telling me that ain't bothering you, Red?" Since he wasn't gonna do a damn thing about it I stormed over to Paulo and stood below his ladder.

"Come on, give it up, you're doing our heads in!" I shouted as loud as I could. "There must be something else you could be doing?" He twisted his body round and smiled through rotting enamel. I don't think he had ever used a toothbrush in his entire life.

"Ugh, that's gross!"

Kira joined me and covered her mouth.

Still on the ladder, Paulo smiled.

"No like?"

"Like what?" I shrugged.

"The new roof..."

Kira stepped closer and squinted.

"That's a window frame."

"What is frame?"

I knew he was going to be hard work.

"Look," I pleaded, "we have headaches and you're making it worse. Please just stop the banging for today – and tomorrow."

"Yeah, we're dying over there," Kira pointed to where Red was lying. "Go pick some magic mushrooms or something."

Raising his bottom lip over his top one, Paulo made a weird face before showing off the awful aging teeth again. He paused, descended from the ladder, took the tin of paint I'd previously used for the sign up the top and began to splash the edges of his frame. I was glad Fin hadn't returned, things were bad enough without having to have a conversation with someone sensible.

By sunset my skin was crawling. I was hungry, but I wasn't. My body needed food, but I didn't. I wanted to wash, but the thought of water suddenly made me cringe. I swung till the hammock snapped. From the floor, I watched Red storm to the cabin and begin to take it apart.

"There's gotta be one more fucking hit!"

He dragged the blankets out and shook them hard. Finding nothing, he stamped on them.

"Oye, we gotta sleep on those!"

I got up and grabbed them.

"Do I look like I care?"

"When do you ever fucking care!"

Confronting Red wasn't easy. His eyes were those of a psycho and his breathing was so fast I thought he was either gonna punch me or pass out. Kira tried to talk to him, but they just ended up having another row. Watching him dismantle the place piece by piece really pissed me off. Not for any particular reason but because everything was irritating and totally irrational. He ransacked everything right down to the mattresses, furious at finding nothing he started to unscrew the floorboards. I suddenly wished Fin would return and sock him one, make him stop and sit still so we could all be sick in silence. But he didn't and Red didn't stop. Sick, and sick of watching, I made off up the track. Knowing there would be warmth and the possibility of a puff, Red didn't hang about too long.

"Wait up! If there's anything going at the fire I want

some."

Red was beginning to unnerve me, so when Kira caught me up I felt better. I didn't know which way I was heading at first, so I just followed my feet. The moon broke through showering the darkness with streaks of light that seemed to laugh at the pain. With each step it felt as if I had weights tied to my ankles. I wanted to give up, lie down, and stay exactly where I fell, but the thought of rotting with the worms forced me on.

Twenty minutes later, flames appeared in the sky. As we grew closer we could hear the hissing of wood. The nearer we got, the more apparent the miserable scene became. Everyone we knew was there, plus a whole lot of folk that we didn't know. A fire the size of a car seemed to be comforting the whole island. Searching for answers, gaunt faces darted about with the flames. Their pain, like ours, hovered like smoke in the air. Many hung their heads, chanting for food, ships, and water. The island was running out of everything and everyone was either withdrawing or hungry. Hovering some feet from them all, we watched the strongest gather wood to burn. As we moved closer, two lads barged past us with half a trunk that they threw on, feeling the heat, my shivering bones began to feel better.

As we walked closer to the fire, a cold hand touched mine and made me jump, a guy wearing a stripy jumper handed me the dregs of a beer. I sipped in the hope of relief, but it might as well have been water. The icy stares and pale faces gave me the creeps. It was the most unsociable gathering in the world, a fucking zombie movie.

"Fucking woman…!" I heard someone yell. "This island's never gone dry of anything before, if a ship don't come soon, there will be nothing, not even water!"

I turned to my left, where I saw a guy sitting cross-legged.

"You know Imelda!" he shouted at me. "She's a bitch – a fucking bitch, ya hear?"

"Ignore him," Kira brushed against me. "Can't you see? He's lost it."

I looked across the fire, where I caught sight of Kitch; fuelled with anger, he charged our way. He shoved me to his left before throwing a high kick at Red's chest.

"Hope you're fucking pleased with yourself!" Red stumbled back, but managed to stay on his feet. Kitch walked towards him, shaking his head. What came next was harsh and swift. Raising his leg, Kitch swept Red's arm in one swift move.

I think we all heard the break. It was like the snapping of a small branch, and the screaming wasn't going to stop for a long time. It took minutes for energies to clash and opinions to lash. I ran to Red and stood over him with several others who'd got up to help. He wriggled a while, then lay still because of the pain that movement inflicted. Kitch cupped his head with his hands and cussed the winds. I felt afraid and confused; I think we all did.

Two Americans set about making a wooden sling. I

watched as they stripped the bark with pen knives. A Dutchman offered his shirt for the sling, but the Yanks insisted that their belts would be better. Sliding the flat wood under the arm was the easy bit. Tying it was another matter.

The first Yank knelt down and leaned over Red, pushing his belt under the wood and around his arm, the Yank spoke.

"I'm going to count to three."

"Let's do it in one," the second Yank said, "too much pain and he'll faint. We can't carry him for long."

As they counted, fear like I'd never seen before crept into Red's face. As the sling came together, his screaming shot through our ears like darts. The Yanks stood him up and signalled for us to lead the way. Desperate not to touch the hanging limb, Red dragged his feet every inch of the way. The torture on his face gave me goose bumps, way out of my depth I just kept going in the hope we would all wake up. With adrenaline racing, it seemed to take only moments to get back. Fin must have heard the wailing long before our silhouettes were visible. One by one the lanterns were lit, a visible stream of light showed the way to the bar where more lanterns were oiled and fired up. Charging towards us, Fin was furious, but turned and led the way into the cabin. Red let out a huge cry as they laid him on the first bed they came to. After that, he went out like a light.

"Who did it?" asked Fin.

"Kitch..."

All speaking at once we sounded muffled.

"I know he's anti this and that, but this!"

Upset and furious, Fin slapped the wall.

"I heard there's a medical hut here somewhere."

It was the first thing either of the Yanks had said since we had all left the fire.

"If there was anything of use there … well it's gone," I said. "Red and Kayden robbed it last week."

Kira sat down and lit five fags in one go.

"It's gonna hurt him twice as much when the cold turkey kicks in."

She handed the Camels out and squeezed her eyes shut.

"Bloody drugs," Fin shook his head and kissed his teeth. "I should have known by the atmosphere the other night. The guy's a bloody black belt, but I never thought he'd use it to break anyone. Best start praying for a ship!"

"You mean there ain't one?" Shocked, I stood up.

"It ran out of supplies a few miles back, I had to pay a private boat to get me here. But even if you had the fare, he ain't fit to island hop. I'll take him," Fin continued, "but only by ship."

Sweatbox

The morning stank. Flies buzzed around unwashed flesh, and the heat was beginning to cook up quite a stench. Nothing could have prepared me for the selfishness invading my body. Instead of feeling the sympathy I normally would towards Red, I felt only irritation at his cries. I could hear the Yanks trying to calm him amid the pain, but they weren't having much luck. I put my hands over my ears, but it wasn't going to stop – not until Fin's ship arrived, and even then it wasn't going to stop us from entering the black hole of pain we were all scheduled for.

Opposite me, Kira sat in silence, her attention concentrated solely on the flies crawling along the wall. Every so often, she managed to swat one with an old paper she'd rolled up.

Lying back down, the pillow and mattress thumped together as I hit them. Searching for precious stones that didn't exist, the seven dwarfs were inside my head with their hammers and chisels. I wanted them to discover the diamonds and treasure so they would stop, but they kept banging, and I knew they weren't going to leave for quite some time. I was cringing and flinching at any little thing – all I wanted was to climb the walls, crawl in with the geckos, shed my skin, and die in private.

After swatting several flies, Kira reached for a pair of string sandals and mumbled something about a bellyache. The sandals kept loosening each time she stood. In the end, she threw them at the wall and went in bare feet. Outside, I heard the Yanks saying goodbye to her. I didn't want them to leave because I didn't know what to do for Red and his escalating pain. Getting up, my bladder began to beep, knowing I wasn't gonna make it outside I grabbed a bucket and peed. The biggest window was in Red's room, poking my head round the door, I was relieved to see him still asleep. Outside I could see the Yanks growing smaller and smaller as they hit the outgoing track. I'd never seen them before the night of the fire and figured I probably never would again. Needing to empty the bucket, I opened the window and hurled the contents outside. Unfortunately, Kira was on her way back and it caught and drenched her arm, within seconds obscenities flew towards me.

"Watch where you're fucking emptying out!"

The fucks she fired into the air reached and woke Red. Seeing him mumble for help, I crawled towards the bunk and rested my head against the bed. Blood had stained the sheets, and shit dribbled down the wood. His arm was still tied to the splint and all in all he looked a crumpled mess. He'd torn the skin on something during the fall, which accounted for the blood.

"I need a drink …"

He pointed to an empty can. Outside thankfully, Fin had filled the other water bottles before going on a walkabout. On her way in Kira grabbed a bottle and brought it inside with her.

We tried to communicate but, no matter how anything was put, it was of little interest, more an irritation than anything else. With Kira's help, I lifted Red's head and held the bottle to his mouth. As he drank, water dribbled down the sides of his mouth, soaking his hair and the top sheets. His eyes shone with growing pain, and the smell made me gag. I put him down, lit a cigarette and held it to his mouth. Taking a swig of water myself, I felt the fur and slime in my own mouth wash away.

"Get the rum!" Red groaned, rolling his eyes and gesturing towards his pillows. Underneath them lay a pig skin pouch that contained warm rum. We took it in turns to provide Red with rum and smokes, until the effort it took him to participate sent him back to the dropout zone.

While Kira searched for Fin's rum barrel I dragged my legs back to bed. Finally, she returned from the bar and handed me a full pouch. I drank great mouthfuls of the stuff, while trying not to throw up. I continued to smoke until my chest hurt and my fingers matched the orange top I wore. My hands played havoc with the covers until I had made a thick dreadlock. Feeling as hot as the sun, I kicked the covers onto the floor, whereupon a moment later, I was cold, and pulled one back over me. Inside my head was an earthquake that came and went and a freight train slowly but surely began to roll into my central brain. It was the same for us all – the cruellest of pain beneath stinking, damp blankets.

My insides felt so loose I thought they would drop out if I got up, but the thought of sleeping in my own shit only brought more mental torture. Eventually, I decided to force my way to the cesspit and lifted the lid. Flies deafened me with their buzzing, and the sight of shit made me heave. The necessity of crouching on my ankles caused the pus from the wounds on my thighs to ooze out. The mozzie bites were sore and ugly, which was exactly how I felt. Not wanting to wake Red, I tiptoed through his part of the cabin; as I did I heard a trickling sound. Still asleep, Red was pissing himself. I knew that by the end of the day the smell was going to be toxic so I fetched some of the sacking Fin had collected, and placed it on the floor below the bed.

Some hours later, there was the sound of Jet barking and I knew Fin was on his way back. I heard the sound of his boots as he reached the door, which he tied open, and I heard him pour some water into a bucket, the sound of a mop brushed against the wood, and a few seconds later the light smell of washing suds floated past. When he'd finished, he entered our end of the cabin.

I sat up to see Fin find his stool and stand on it. He reached for the hook in the ceiling beam where he hung a string of fish, finished fiddling he turned to me.

"Has Red been sleeping?"

"Yeah, he's been sleeping, had a drink and that was it."

"I searched for a ship while I was fishing, but there's nothing on the horizon yet." Fin tightened the knot around the fish, and stepped down from the stool.

"The heat will dry these out. Just break them off and eat them as and when you want. How're the legs?"

I folded the sheet back and saw that the wounds had worsened since the sickness set in and were really pus-filled in places. Fin turned to glance at Kira. Her hair was soaked and stuck to her face.

"You guys have got it bad? How about you try some bread?"

Fin took one of the rolls from his bag and handed it to me before going to do more chores. Due to my shrunken stomach, the crusts were like cardboard and just caused more cramps. I offered the roll to Kira. Sweating profusely, she fumbled for a smoke, which helped to mask the smell of bad breath and body odour.

I could hear Fin fishing for water in the big holding drums. I watched him shower the grass plants until everyone had had its fill. Because he was a permanent fixture on the island, Fin had a good supply of water and more contacts than most. There was something comforting about Fin's presence. It didn't ease the pain, but it certainly brought an air of security. In the bar, Fin put music on. I lay listening to every word Sting sang. I wanted to put a message in my bottle, a message for help, heroin, and freedom. Something that said were fucked up, find us if you can'.

On the second day, voices I knew but could no longer place drifted in and out of my hearing. The word 'ship' may have passed me by, but then it could have been 'shit.'

The loud screams and the sound of the buckle dragging along the wooden floor confirmed that it was ship and that Red was being moved. I tried to get up to see what was going on, but my legs felt paralysed, dead weights that were unable to function. I forced myself onto them and managed to get a quick glimpse of Red being carried away before I fell down.

As the cries faded up the track, I drifted back off. Heroin filled my dreams, calling and dancing everywhere I went. It was on every street corner, in every shop window, and outside every school. Natives were selling it from the woods, and sailors from their ships. Tempted and teased from every angle I eventually woke around dusk. Full of panic, prickly heat irritated my skin. Jet was on the end of my bunk; his panting sounded a thousand times louder than normal. I looked to my left and saw that Kira had lit one of the oil lamps; sitting next to it she was emptying the ash tray of decent-sized butts and splitting them open, she fumbled to make full-sized smokes from them. She shivered as she pulled an old blanket around her shoulders; lighting up she pulled hard before passing it to me.

"Least Red's out of it now," she said.

"Where…?"

"Capital – with Fin, I think."

"His prayers were answered then."

"Suppose …"

"D'ya think supplies came too?"

"Who knows, anything other than pain will do at the moment."

Knowing how alone we were and how dark it would soon be, I crept in with Kira and cuddled up to her. Occasionally twirling, the silver scales on the fish sparkled. They reminded us of homemade wind-chimes – only they didn't chime, just hummed real bad each time a breeze entered.

Jet's presence made us both feel better and sleep became easier. By the third morning I was starving, stinking, and unable to sleep any more.

"Come on," I said, "let's get some air."

At first my feet struggled to take my weight, and I wobbled a bit as before. But, with a little determination and some encouragement from Jet, I was outside where I waited for Kira. Once she had managed to tie her sandals, she joined me. The walking seemed to go on forever, and the tropical temperatures did nothing to ease the pimples on my skin. We played *I spy* along the way, but I gave it up when Kira used the leaves for a third time. We took a shortcut, and the shrubbery scratched and tore at our legs as we passed. By the time we reached the end tracks, our legs looked as if someone had drawn on them.

Finally, we broke through the trees and stood before the ocean. The waves looked more like sheets of ice than the oasis they were. Kira counted to three and made a run for it. She stood waist-high in the water, then hunched and dunked herself. A moment later, her tanned face surfaced white as a ghost. Gasping for air, she turned.

"C'mon, it's not too bad if you're quick." With that, she was gone again.

I knew I'd have to brave it. My hunger was overwhelming, but I knew that to present myself to anyone, anywhere, in my current state of stink was totally unacceptable. As I waded in, shock waves penetrated my body. Standing chest-high, I felt like a giant sea-sponge full of dents and holes borne there by life. As cold as I felt, I let the salt and seaweed purify my skin and sores. I could see the floating bar a hundred feet or so away. It was quieter than usual – just some big guy sitting on the edge. Under the waves, near my feet, were star fish I'd never seen before. I was totally engrossed in them when Kira crept up behind me. After making me jump, she waded back to shore with a smirk on her face. I shook myself down and caught her up.

"Dunno about you, but I'm starving, looks like he is too."

I turned to Jet, and called him. His tail propelled in the air like a whip. "You hungry, boy…?" Jet jumped up and down and tried to stand on his back legs. "Wonder if the ships brought anything?"

"There's only one way to find out."

Up and on her feet, Kira scanned the beach for the nearest hut. There was nothing on the visible horizon, so we began to walk. Melons at the 'White Sail' were a good sign so we bought two and continued inland to see what else had arrived. The first hut had crisps, cakes, and cigarettes. The owner, who was still trying to organise himself, invited us around the back of his little shop hut where opened boxes sat strewn on the sand. Some were full of biscuits, others held tins and packet foods, but the biggest luxury was the tea and toothpaste that had arrived. We bought what we could carry and made our way back. Starving, on arrival we opened a tin of corned beef and mixed it with some butter beans. We shared it with Jet and ate well for the first time in days.

Three cigarettes later, I was feeling the cramps again. Having reached a sleepless stage of cold turkey, and unable to purchase so much as an aspirin anywhere, I was feeling demented all over again. Depression engulfed me as though someone had injected it there, and with nothing but nicotine at hand, it is safe to say I became a very heavy smoker. Kira searched the bar for something stronger than beer, but the rum had run dry. Climbing onto the bar she had a mad singing moment.

"The good old boys were drinking whisky and rye, singing this'll be the day that I die. This'll be the day that I die."

She gave it up after a few wiggles and sat down, then, reaching back to the fridge top, she pulled two beers towards her, one of which she handed to me. My taste buds were up the wall, and the beer tasted the way I imagined piss to be. I watched Kira poke between the bar slats with a small stick.

Apart from the odd pebble, it was mostly sand that surfaced.

"Nothing's gonna touch this bastard, is it?" She gave me a weird look followed by one of her saucy grins. "Who d'ya think thought up the name 'cold turkey'?"

"Dunno," I said, as I made my way towards the cesspit. "But whoever did was a complete cunt!"

As I arrived there, I pinched my nose together. Urine hummed on the fading heat waves, and insects danced to the smell of shit. I was squatting with my eyes closed when I heard Kira scream with delight.

"It's hash…!" She raved. "Found some bloody hash!"

Jumping up, I headed towards her.

"Probably from when Red cut up for the cakes," I yelled, "do we have skins?"

"If we ain't, well, just eat it." Kira dug into the depths of her denim pocket, and found some scrunched-up papers.

It didn't cure us – just gave us two smokes that induced instant short-term sleep. Each time we woke up, we tried playing *I spy* again, but using Jet, the lamps, and the fish over and over again was as bad as cold turkey itself. Lying awake in the dark irritated me as much as having no drugs. I could sense that Kira was also still awake so I asked her what it was like going with girls. I knew when she got up to join me that I was about to find out. I wasn't totally against the idea, men were mean and she was a great-looking girl. She put her arm around me and gave me a soft kiss that led to another and another, comfortable I kissed her back. She ran her fingers through my hair and continued down my back. I'd been emotionally numb for so long, she had no problem in stirring me up. I could almost see the stars explode above my head. Satisfied, we both slept well for the first time in ages. I woke around six to the sound of squawking. I peeled Kira's arms away from me and went to the window where my jaw dropped. "What the fuck! Get a load of this."

Paulo's hut was set at an angle on the small plot of land, but not so far away that we couldn't see him holding a hen at arm's length and waist high while his hips juggled an invisible hoop.

"It ain't possible, is it?"

Kira joined me, "seeing is believing," she covered her mouth.

"I knew he was weird but that's below the belt, I mean, what can he get out of it?"

Kira turned to me with one of her sarcastic grins.

"Cock-tucky chicken…!"

I laughed like I hadn't in quite a while.

"Don't order me any more omelettes!"

"Take it chicken's off the menu, too?" She smiled.

We watched him toss the hen aside and search for his forest bag. Hooking it over his shoulder, he made off as though nothing had happened.

"Well, now my mind's been expanded on man's capabilities, I think I need a walk."

I pulled a semi-clean top over my head, fumbled for

change and embraced the morning with Jet in tow. Nearing Mallie's we stopped to ask her if she was up for some breakfast.

Mallie wasn't used to being up early. Grumpy as hell, she heated some bread and cut cheese from a newly arrived block. Remembering the night when we'd first arrived, my thoughts turned to Kayden. I wasn't even sure if he knew about Red. Approaching us with two banana shakes, Mallie slammed them down and went off in a huff. Bread and cheese still on the side, Kira got up and grabbed it. Half an hour later, we paid and rolled a bit further on. My social skills were shit, but my legs still worked.

As we neared the top of the beach track, the sun grew warmer and Jet began to bark at the sound of oncoming hooves.

"What the hell…"

I looked down the track and was shocked to see a fat guy spurring a small horse forward with a stick. As they grew closer, we saw just how much weight was suffocating the pony. Kira stepped into its path, and waved her arms.

"Slow down, you fat fucker."

Refusing to acknowledge her, the guy continued to scream and spur the poor pony forward, forcing us either side of the path as he barged past. I caught my breath and stood up straight.

"Place gets crazier by the minute!"

Jet tried to tackle the pony's heels, calling him off we

continued to the shore. The ship had brought much, including nets that fishermen were trying out. There was no floating bar – just a few swimmers soaking in the sea and sun before it rose properly.

Kira took a stick and drew silly pictures in the sand to pass time. "What do you wanna do now?" She asked.

"Walk, I suppose. See what the day has to offer."

As we rounded the bend in the beach, we saw spots of colour set along the sand. Walking closer we saw the shapes were actually sails drying in the sun. A few hundred yards on, a surfing shed appeared. We could see all sorts laid out, and wandered around them all. Kira lifted one of the boards…

"Go on, I dare ya."

"You can do better than that." A Swede left the surfing shed, closed the door and came towards us.

"Windsurfed before?"

"No," I said, "but I got a feeling I'm about to try."

"Only if you want…"

He stood the board upright and threaded the rope to the top of the pole, then pulling on it hard, the sail stood upright.

"There ya go. It's a perfect breeze today, this one's on me."

While he prepared a second sail for Kira, I made my way towards the sea. The board was heavy, so I was glad when the sea took the weight from me. As I waded in, goose bumps popped up like acne. I knew my body temperature was still up the creek, but didn't want to let the experience pass me by.

With a little encouragement from Jet I kept going till up to my chest. Shivering I sat on the board, trying to stand on it was quite another thing. My feet slipped each time I tried. As with any kind of sport, the key to success is balance, and I had none. I felt Kira approaching. Having already gone down twice, she was cussing and cursing the sea.

Trying not to laugh, I forced the sail up and dug my heels into the back of the board, leaned back and concentrated. It was on that board that I found freedom for the first time in a very long time. The breeze blew over my belly and sea salt through my senses, lifting my spirit the natural world made me glad to be alive. Of course, the fall into cold water brought me back to earth, but the experience would never die.

"That was all right, that was."

Kira passed me, skimmed the ocean and made good progress before hitting the fall. I clapped as she went down and began to make my way back to shore. I'd just joined Jet when I heard Kira splashing about. She shoved the board onto the sand and joined us. Raving about the ride, she beamed for the first time in a long time.

"You know, I like it here!" she went on. "But money's gonna force us back."

She had a good point, one I'd been trying to ignore for lots of reasons.

"Was fun?" The Swede cast a shadow.

"Brilliant." I looked up and smiled at him.

"If you come back, I'll do you a discount."

"I'll keep that in mind."

I shook his hand and thanked him for the freebie. We were about halfway when we could hear the sound of Bob Marley. Jamming along the beach, we stopped at the 'White Sail' where we joined Muzz and Emelio. It was the first time we'd seen them since the fire. Being friends with both Red and Kitch made things difficult for them. But, no matter how any of us put it, we all struggled to justify what Kitch had done. Changing the subject to heroin seemed appropriate since we all wanted some and nobody had any. We teased one another about past highs and lows, laughing about the day we'd all gone sand-sieving under the wooden cabin. Bringing up the state of Red that day Emelio began to chuckle.

"So, you did notice," I laughed.

"Of course…!" Muzz cut in. "But we had heroin on our minds. We did laugh later though, Kayden wore enough to paint a bus, took him a week to realize."

"What, you've seen him?" Kira enquired.

"Yeah, he went to sleep his cold turkey away in one of the hollows. We were at the sand hut when he came to get some food. That's when we just had to tell him."

"Is he still there?" I asked.

"Dunno, he mentioned the falls, it's a good place to freshen up. Hey, while I remember, there's a proper party on the hill Saturday night."

"Saturday…?"

I felt slightly embarrassed as I asked Emilio what day it was.

"I think today is Thursday." Heading off he looked back. "So, we see you Saturday?"

"Maybeeee..."

Jet took off after them, and tugged at their heels, covered in sand his snout looked speckled and silly. The walk back was easier than earlier, arriving at Fin's, we heard Paulo before we saw him. He'd just finished banging a second window frame together. We sat down on the cabin steps while we watched him paint it. Afterwards he took a pan and filled it with water and rice. Instead of doing the usual exit into the woods, he lit a stove and watched it cook. When it had boiled he divided soup slop into two bowls, came towards us and put one down for Jet.

"Fin comes soon. You'll see."

He then wandered off to the water containers and checked they were full. Kira sat upright, shuddering.

"How does he know when Fin's back?"

"He doesn't. He's just making conversation with something other than his hens."

Paulo then waded into the shrubs, carrying a big bucket, and began to spray the grass plants. I'd had enough action for one day, going inside I fell asleep.

I woke, startled and surprised to find Red standing before me. He had a peachy glow about him and had gained a few pounds that filled his hollow cheeks. His arm had been neatly plastered and tied up, and for once, he looked genuinely happy.

"I'm surprised you came back, with Kitch still around."

"He left when we did. Last I saw of him was on the banana boat making his way back to Germany. Besides, there wasn't a lot I could do in that state if he did want another pop at me – was there? Don't suppose you got much use for these now, 'ave ya?"

Red dug into his pocket, and pulled out some painkillers. Disappointed I didn't need them, I shook my head. Kira sat up and joined us.

"So how was the hospital?"

"A bit overcrowded from the street casualties, but, in my state, anywhere offering relief was good."

"Talking of relief, you should have seen Paulo day before yesterday!"

Red sat down and listened to what we had seen.

"You're away from civilization, now!" He laughed.

"Yeah, but shagging poultry must be shite!" Kira went on.

"I wouldn't know, would I?" On hearing a loud thud, we all turned to face the door. Seeing Fin was less fun than we had expected, half- smiling, he cut the fish down and disappeared.

"What's with him?" I asked.

"Girlfriend's knocked up and giving him a hard time. He don't wanna live in Manila, and she don't 'ere. Threatened him with all sorts, she has."

"Like what?"

"Dunno, but it's not good. Let's get a fire going, burn some food, maybe it'll bring Fin out of his shell."

By the time we'd finished, the stars were peeping through the sky. Fin, seeing our efforts, gave up the bad mood, removed himself from the grass plants, and brought some of it over to us.

Once relaxed, he began to talk. After the second joint there was no stopping him.

"I'm not like other guys who go to Manila and then leave their women. I just don't want to live in the city. If she'd only give it a chance here, I'm sure she'd like it."

"Did you tell her that?" I asked nervously.

"Of course, but she's confused about lots of stuff. Her parents, for one thing, expect her to work in that bar to keep them; they make her feel so damn guilty for wanting a life. It's all wrong – especially now they have another house and don't need her as much anymore."

He got up and began to do pointless tasks before disappearing again. There was nothing any of us could do, so we just carried on smoking. We spent the rest of the night scaring the shit out of each other. Trees made good triffids, and bushes, great ghosts.

Tripping

A storm had been brewing all day. As night closed, the threatening thunder and sea breezes brought our imaginary stuff to life. Legs jutted from tree trunks and twigs seemed to grow fingers that curled and wriggled towards us. An owl swooped from a tree and flung itself onto the ground; I didn't think it was real until the faint squeal of a mouse confirmed otherwise. Scared shitless, we retired to the cabin where I lit an oil lamp and candle.

"Why both?" asked Red.

I walked away from the candle and climbed onto the bunk. Red's face looked rounder in the dark, more as it was when his passport photo had been taken.

"In case one runs out before the other. Get some kip."

Careful not to lie on his arm, Red doubled his good side up as a pillow. Likewise Kira too had no trouble in sleeping, but Red's snoring was loud and drove me mad. Every so often, I pinched his nose, but it only stopped the noise for a few seconds. I was about to put a peg over his nose, when I heard Fin approach with Jet. Standing in the doorway, he paused before pulling his boots off.

"It's going to be a breaker."

I pulled a face. He shoved me up and snuggled in.

"The storm – it's been preparing itself all day. Any minute now, you'll see."

"How d'ya know?"

"Because the air's moist, thicker than normal."

Sure enough the first drops fell slowly then gathered speed. As their weight increased they fell like a billion bombs, and the thunder grew so loud that it woke the others and sent Jet dashing for cover under one of the beds.

"Bloody hell," lights burned out, Red struggled up onto his good side, "I'd forgotten how rough they got."

He swung himself round, pulling his feet away from the end of the bed. "Shit, we gotta leak!"

Shaking himself down Red moved away from the rear end of the bunk.

Fin sat up, "Paulo should have sealed this roof, there's enough bloody tar in store."

It was dark but as lightning shot us a bolt of light the bucket beside his boots became visible. I held it under the rain while Fin tried to block the hole and stop the rain from coming in.

"Are they usually this harsh?" Kira asked as she lit a cigarette.

Fin looked down.

"Always. You want to be here during the rainy season; it's like this for three months."

"No wonder you need so much gear," she went on. "It's miserable."

"Storm's good. The ground needs nourishing. Everything will grow now."

Having stuffed a scarf between the rafters, Fin hammered a nail into the roof and hooked the bucket there. I jumped off the bed and lit the last candle; then, turning to Fin, I spoke.

"Do you think you'll ever go home?"

"Will people ever change?" He asked me.

I shook my head.

"Then you have your answer."

The rain was harsh. It sounded like a million small spoons beating an African drum, and I had a horrible vision of the roof caving in and carrying us all out to sea. Our candle was nearly done and the reserves were at the bar. Even if it was possible to battle the elements, I don't think any of us would have made it without being flattened to the ground. As the candle burned out, we huddled together for the first time. I could hear the waves dancing and beating the shore as though it had done them a great injustice.

"Where do you think the abos take shelter?" I asked Fin.

"Probably amongst the larger trees, some have hollows big as tents, you know."

"And Paulo…?" I felt fascinated by the whole ordeal.

"It doesn't bother him." Raising his arm Fin pointed. "Probably right over there snuggled up asleep."

We took it in turns to empty the bucket before giving it up as a bad job.

Eventually the constant rain created a pattern of sound that sent us all back to sleep. It was Red who woke us with one of his yells. He'd put weight on his arm, crushing it in pain. Fin jumped up and felt for Red's jacket, on finding his painkillers, he popped three out and fed them to him.

"You're gonna have to be more careful, my man!"

"Yeah do," Kira said, "'cos believe me, there's nothing available when they're gone!"

I could see that irritation was mixing with his pain, but instead of releasing it, Red sat back and closed his eyes. By now, the rain had subsided, so Fin opened up, whereupon Jet tore past him and into the puddles. I lent Fin a hand to help him balance while he took down the full bucket. Outside, everything had been replenished, the scary tree trunks displayed a beautiful reddish brown and the waters gathered along the bark were almost two-tone. When I cast my eyes further upwards I saw leaves glowing with a richness I'd only ever seen in springtime. The smell of ground minerals made the morning the best yet. Fin reached for the heavens as he threw Jet a ball, when he returned Kira appeared and tackled him for it. Five minutes later, I watched Red join in. He kicked the ball hard across the land. Fin tore after it, racing Jet across the clearing and into the shallow undergrowth. I smiled after him, feeling strong for the first time since the sickness had set in; it seemed that the storm had given a new lease of life to more than just nature. I decided the beach would be a good place to explore – see what the weather had washed up and left behind. I knew we would need breakfast so combining the two journeys seemed sensible. I knew Red wouldn't be up for it, and that Fin had a few chores to do, so

I went with Kira and Jet. The sea was calm after its heavy night and looked beautiful. While Jet feasted on the fish left behind, we examined some of the strange shells. There were so many to choose from, we found ourselves spoilt for choice. As we walked along, we stepped over seaweed, sea-cucumbers, starfish and bright stones. We came across a dead lionfish, It was so pretty I wanted to keep it, but knowing it might still be poison we pushed it back to sea. When we turned round we began to collect unusual shells and some of the seaweed. Further down the beach, Jet barked frantically. Catching him up, we watched a spiky shell that he was sniffing crawl across the sand. We followed its giant legs back to sea, and decided to join it for a swim. Jet didn't usually swim too far out, but the crab had excited him and he swam further than normal. Once my feet were off the sand, I began to tread water with him. Taking it in turns with Kira we held onto his collar and let him plough through the water with us. Jet went so fast he nearly swam into an oncoming canoe. It wasn't unusual for folk to venture in and out of the place, especially now the supply ship had been and gone, however, it was unusual for females to travel alone. The dark-haired woman had a blank stare that was a bit unnerving. As I trod water, I watched the woman near the shores where Cameron and what looked like the Swedes stood waving at us, swimming towards them I noticed the boat turn to the left but thought no more of it. Jet drenched Cameron as he jumped out of the sea.

"Hey," he said, "I heard Red is back."

I nodded while shivering at the same time.

"And the arm, good, I hope?"

"Yeah," Kira said. "It's as good as it gets." Cameron stepped backwards and gave her the thumbs up.

"Now the bad time's gone, time for a good one."

Muzz, agreeing with him, took some cigarettes from a packet and held them out. Emelio lit them all and put one in my mouth.

"What say we all head back and surprise them?"

Already barking, Jet ran up front. Cameron took a ball from his bag and held it up.

"Since we're all sober, how about it?"

We dribbled the ball, and tackled along the tracks till we reached the sign that I had put at the top of Fin's place.

Sneaking down the track, we jumped out on them. Red and Fin were thrilled to see the lads. Their presence seemed to do Fin good. After they had all scribbled on Red's plaster, Cameron began to kick the ball again. Fin showed off his skills in tackling him and when he retrieved the ball he booted it hard, away from Cameron. We clapped him and watched them for half an hour or so. Eventually Fin stopped and raised his arms.

"I got just the challenge!"

He disappeared into the cabin and, returned with a long rope. Passing Red, he smiled.

"But not for you, my friend."

He marched towards the giant tree at the centre of his holding and attempted to throw the rope into the air.

"There's no way that's happening," Cameron shouted. "We need a climber."

Cameron then collected several twigs, clenched them all together and squashed his hand shut.

"Smallest one goes first."

He held them out and waited while we took them. Fin drew long, then Kira, Cameron, and Emelio. Muzz, having lost the draw, hooked the rope around his shoulder and began to bear-hug the tree to the top. He got halfway up before his hands became sore and forced him down. Emelio, taking the rope, rubbed his hands in the earth and made it to the top where he tied one end around a strong branch and lowered the other half to the lads, who knotted it up. It was a great swing, but we had to climb the tree in order to qualify to use it. One by one, the lads cheered each other to the top, then came my turn.

Grudgingly, I began the climb. My fear of heights kicked in around a third of the way up, but slowly I pushed on. Encouragement from the others helped me to keep going. It was while I had stopped for air that I noticed the dark-haired woman I'd seen in the boat making her way down the track, eyes wild her hands were clutched tightly around a large-mouthed jar.

"Who's that?" I yelled, pointing towards her. Raising their hands to block out the sun, the others all turned and squinted her way.

"Oh no..!" Fin yelled.

He turned and marched up the track to meet her. Frozen to the tree, I watched with the others as the distance between him and the wild woman closed. To begin with, there were only moving heads. I saw her thrust the jar towards his waist, but Fin pushed it back. Within minutes, the language became loud and vicious. Fin didn't usually swear, but the 'fucks' rolled down the track as the storm had previously done. Clutching his sides and shaking his head, Fin marched to and fro waving his hands at her. Finally, he reached for the sky, fell to his knees and clamped his head.

"I never thought she'd come here."

It was Red.

"Who...?" Kira and the others glanced his way.

"Obria, his woman, I met her once while in the city. She came with Fin to the hospital the day I was discharged."

"What the fuck's she up to?"

Creasing his forehead, Cameron made corrugated rivets there while furiously tapping the ball.

"I think I know," Red stepped back. "She was making a song and dance about being pregnant in the capital."

"So what the fuck is she doing?"

Cameron booted the ball so hard it skimmed the near shrubbery as it passed.

"Dunno, but whatever it is, don't look good, does it?"

Obria placed the bottle on the ground and turned to leave.

Still on his knees, Fin cussed her in Italian.

"I don't think I wanna see this," Red pulled his hat over his eyes.

Shaking his head furiously, Cameron lit up.

"Me neither. I've heard of this sort of thing and it ain't nice!"

I began to climb down, jumping the last few feet, when I joined the others. Though Fin had his back to us, it was obvious by the uncontrollable movement of his body that he was crying.

"We can't just leave him there," Muzz said. "Someone's gotta go."

We stared at one another, looking for a volunteer. Muzz spat hard and headed up the track, stopping a few feet from where Fin knelt. He threw his arms in the air and stared at the ground. Moments later, lips hard pressed together, he marched back.

"Well?" Kira whispered.

"It's a fucking foetus!" Muzz snapped.

Motionless we watched Muzz storm into the woods, where he disappeared.

In that moment I don't even think the storm would have moved us. Then Cameron let rip.

"Fucking whore…!"

He turned towards the woods and went after Muzz.

I wanted to say something to ease Fin's misery, but what was there, 'Oh, sorry your girlfriend's a psycho, a cold cow, a twisted bitch?' Where would one stop? Besides, it's bad enough having shite memories to carry through life without the images to go with them. There was nothing anyone could say or do to ease his pain. It was a time that only he could deal with. Obria had set out to blow Fin's mind. Instead, she'd done us all. Kira wanted to go after her, give her a slap, a few digs just for the hell of it, but, as we pointed out, that wasn't going to change how Fin was feeling – not now.

One by one we trailed into the woods, we heard Muzz cussing Obria before we saw him. A few yards on, we entered a small area of fallen logs the large trunks the storm had taken down reminded me of a wooden Stonehenge.

"What a fucking sadist! Bitch needs shooting." Muzz didn't look up, just kept talking down to the wood as though he expected an answer.

"Yeah, don't fuck with Filipinos, ain't that what they say?"

Cameron came into the circle from a tree he'd been leaning on, and sat down. Several minutes later smoke rose from where we'd left Fin and the breeze carried the faint smell of something weird our way. The conversation became dull and full of sad speculation. Realising what was going on, I began to gag.

"I'm heading in," said Cameron. "You're welcome at my place, if you want."

Unable to face Fin, we took Cameron up on his offer and followed him into the forest. We ventured further into the woods, where the trees became taller and thicker. Cameron eventually stopped below a giant oak. Inside it was one of the hollows Fin had mentioned during the storm. As I stepped inside it I was amazed at just how big it was. Above, underneath the leaf canopies, I saw a wooden platform that snaked around the whole area. Cameron pulled on a rope ladder and climbed several steps before turning to Red.

"Try it now, if Muzz goes behind ya we can all support you and pull you on your good side."

Red tired around a third of the way up, leaning down, Cameron took hold of his good arm and hauled him up.

I followed Emelio, and began to climb to the top platform. Apart from the twigs and leaves the storm had left the place was real snug, like a giant cup without the handle. Cameron released some branches that he had tied back and opened them up into personal sunshades. As we smoked quietly beneath them, we absorbed sights and sounds of the jungle. I was fiddling with the matches Red had handed me when I felt my fingers brush against something card-like.

"What's this?" I asked him, twirling it around my fingers.

"Acid... Someone in Manila gave it to me. Don't know if it's any good now."

"You sly old dog...!" Muzz took the card from me and felt it.

Ten minutes later, we'd all examined it and were contemplating a chew. If nothing else, it would take our minds away from what we'd just experienced. It was mere cardboard, and a snippet in size, so down it went. Waiting for something to happen, I lit up. I felt nothing for ages but as time passed, I began to feel strange, out of control and totally out of this world. I don't remember getting from Cameron's to the beach bar, but obviously I did because I didn't choke on the beer I drank and people moved when I touched them.

I laughed so much that everyone wanted to know what I'd been drinking, which made me laugh even more. I couldn't see Red or Cameron, but the Swedes and Kira were there. Remembering the party on the mountain, Kira suggested we grab the Swedes and go. The journey was a time tunnel of twisted tracks and crazy conversation. Every now and then, Emelio changed direction until we finally stood at the bottom of a hill that was to become a mountain.

Oblivious of my vertigo, my legs found abnormal strength, and I climbed without hesitation, pulling myself up and up into the darkness of the night. It was steep and rough, but the protruding boulders made great footholds which enabled me to scramble to the top. I felt on top of the world, and, in a sense, I suppose I was. Blurred voices and shadows ahead told me I wasn't alone.

"Over here!" they shouted.

I walked towards the others, and checked out the light. It was like someone was holding a giant torch, wiggling it from side to side, making its flames flicker and bash the streaky sky. As we got nearer, the fire lit the night and most of the surrounding landscape. I could see bodies and shadows moving to the music. As I settled down on my own, I watched the colourful ghosts float towards me in silent slow motion before they disappeared again. The breeze made them graceful and almost alien-like, but I knew they were real because every now and then, I recognized a voice.

It was nice sitting in my own space and if I could have pressed a stop button I would have, for in that moment absolutely nothing in the world mattered. I woke to see orange ashes glowing at me. Like the night, the fire had disintegrated somewhat. Kira approached, puffing slightly from all the dancing she'd been doing. She smiled, held out a hand and pulled me to my feet. We didn't really speak, just began to follow our feet back towards the rock face. It was while we were climbing down that I noticed how steep some of the walls actually were. It was as if a giant had taken a brush and painted perfect white pebbles in places. It was those perfect surfaces that caused us to slip and slide.

"Go on, let go."

I could just make out Emelio in the dawning light. I jumped. Breaking my fall, he checked I was okay before turning to catch Kira. Seeing Muzz, Emelio stepped back and made room for him to land. I turned onto a track and examined the palm trees which ran either side of us. Rich in colour they captivated me. Their coffee-coloured trunks and gorgeous green tops had been perfectly painted by the 'Green Man'. The mass of leaves drooping down from the top of them reminded me of hair. I tied my belt around its middle standing back I thought it looked like Jimmie. Emelio kept giving me strange looks. I wasn't sure if he'd had a blot dot or not, so I just smiled at him.

For some unknown reason, we turned left towards the sound of the sea and answered its call. Black waves on the hazy horizon looked as if they were building themselves up into tidal waves before they roared and dissolved on the sand. A voice echoed through the dawn. At first I thought it was just the wind calling, until the outline of a boat became visible. As we got closer, the voice grew louder.

"Got a hand? I'm sand-locked."

I squinted several times and rubbed my eyes. The morning was waking but the dark still outweighed the light. Standing on the shore, we saw the boat. It was fifty yards or so out. The voice came again. "Can you pull?"

"Throw us a rope!" Muzz shouted back.

It hit the water three or four times before it was within our reach. Muzz made the first move. He waded in, took hold of the rope and called for us to join him. Paddling into the ocean in the semi- darkness wasn't the greatest of experiences. It was pretty freaky standing there half-swallowed by the sea, with our feet sinking into the sand. We leaned back and pulled as hard as we could. Fighting the sand, we tried to pull the boat ashore. Emelio slipped twice before he managed to get a good grip. Shivering like shit we pulled our hardest and gradually felt the sand-lock lift. After that, the boat began to move. Its occupant jumped down as soon as he knew his feet would reach the bottom, and he helped to push the boat to shore. Seeing he was safe, we turned and continued our journey back. The sand bumps, reminding us all of heroin. Grabbing handfuls of it we began to fill our pockets, singing all sorts of songs as we danced across the sand in different directions. Whistling, Muzz captured all our attentions, an arm raised, body poised on one leg he wobbled.

"Who's up for it?"

Within seconds we had all caught on and were raring to catch the invisible ball. Muzz raised his left arm and threw hard; chasing it across the sand, Kira caught it and threw it to Emelio who went down on his knees to catch it. From the ground he threw to me and I back to Kira. Muzz closed in and yelled to her, obliging, she threw hard, to ensure that the ball wasn't lost, Muzz went hard down on his front, skimming the sand he caught it once again.

He shouted my name, I stumbled but managed to catch it, getting up I threw it to Muzz. He raced across the beach, bent, hesitated, and caught again. Knowing it was coming her way and not wanting to break the energy, Kira ran like the wind. We went several rounds before Emelio finally dropped the ball and broke the force. Unable to get the buzz back we began to walk. I think the lads must have chipped off because one minute they were there, and the next it was just Kira and me back at Fin's.

Sweet 'n' Sour

I awoke earlier than usual, eager to absorb some more of the gorgeous green we'd previously seen, I made straight for the window. I sighed.

"Is it all boring?" Kira asked.

Pressing my lips together I nodded in disappointment. The rich, out-of-this-world green had gone. The trees stood still and my pockets contained nothing but sand. Everything, like Fin's place, was mundane, miserable and empty. I pushed the door open and turned.

"I could have sworn Jet was here when we got back."

"Probably was," Kira yawned. "Fin often goes out real early to do his rounds, but after yesterday, he could be anywhere."

"Poor bastard, d'ya think that's the place?" I pointed to a burnt-out circle near the tree we had all been climbing. We made our way over to the spot, where we stood quietly looking over the charred ground. Next to the trunk was a plastic bag; when we opened it we saw it contained the broken bottle. Suddenly startled by a shadow we nearly jumped out of our skins. I swung round, dropping the bag I saw Paulo. Mumbling in a native tongue that neither of us understood, he snatched the bag away from us and strode off into the woods.

"'Morning, to you too..."

A few moments later the words 'pig float' rolled down the track, accompanied by Red and Cameron. I looked at Kira, and raised my eyebrows.

"Sounds as if they're still high…"

"I don't think they did one. There's no way Red could have risked it what with his arm the way it is. Guess he had to sit this one out."

"First time for everything..." I said.

As we watched them close in, the rucksack on Cameron's back became clearer, and confirmed that something was happening. Cameron gazed immediately at the ground and just stared. Standing lopsided, Red smiled.

"Knew you'd find your way back here, have you seen him?"

I shook my head. Cameron reluctantly removed his gaze from the charred circle and gave the perimeter the once-over.

"Not nice," he said. "The beach is pretty mad at the moment. A ship came earlier. Saw it arrive from the tree house. So, you ready to roll?

"You coming…?" I asked.

"I need some stuff the shacks don't stock, you know, soul-saving stuff like books, batteries and muuuussic."

"What about Fin…?"

"I'm sure he'll be fine." Red made his way to the cabin and began to sort stuff out. There wasn't much to take. Most of the stuff we'd brought had been worn to death and needed to be dumped or left. Cameron sat in the doorway and waited while the three of us packed what was worth keeping, and donated what was left to Paulo. We loaded up, and made our final journey through the woods.

The beach was the busiest I'd ever seen it. Desperate to make as much cash as possible, small boats played relay with the waiting folk on shore. People I'd never seen before were waving and calling to the canoe boats. With everyone eager to set foot on the ship it was mayhem. As I stood on that beach, I suddenly had a moment of my own. I didn't really want to leave. I had just got clean and used to the way of life, but I knew we couldn't stay without more money, and Hong Kong was the only place I knew I could make some.

Cameron caught one of the oncoming boats and called to us while he held it still. It was an amazing place, one that would stay with me forever. I couldn't help thinking of Fin and how he must be feeling. But mostly I was gutted not to have been able to say goodbye to him. Ten minutes later, we were bobbing about the ship's flank. Having had some practice on Cameron's rope, Red was able to make the one-armed pulls a bit more easily. While we were waiting for him to reach the top, I was pleased and proud to see Fin appear on the beach with Jet. Using his hand as a telescope, he scanned the water till he found us. He waved furiously, blew kisses and put his thumbs in the air.

"He's a good guy," Cameron winked. "A survivor too, sometimes reliving shit in solitude makes us stronger."

I think I knew what Cameron meant.

"Life's an unpredictable bitch," he continued. "But he looks okay now."

While I wrestled the ropes to the top, I waved a hundred waves. I was standing on the highest rung leaning over the deck, when I saw the others waiting for me.

"It's a fucking madhouse!" I called down.

"That's why they call it the *banana boat!*" Cameron raised his arms for me to jump and stepped forward slightly. Having jolted his sling on the way down we helped Red to readjust it and tie it back into place.

Inside was a mass of crammed congestion, a floating market owned by the Natives, Aborigines and Orientals all squashed together amongst the goods they guarded. Wire baskets of gaggling hens, fish, beans, and beads made a minefield for my feet. I placed one foot carefully in front of the other so as not to offend anyone. I was doing well until a sack of grain fell in front of me, and I tripped on it, which made the sides split scattering some of the lentils. The owner jumped up, shouting obscenities. He held a hand out, haggling, and tried to make me feel guilty. I was grateful for Red's good arm pushing me forward, thus preventing any further unwanted haggling. I breathed a sigh of relief as I reached the stairs. We followed the faded arrows painted on the wall, and turned left at the top. Most of the rooms were already occupied by foreigners who were either sleeping or smoking. We wandered on to the end of the corridor, where we finally found a dorm that still had spaces. The beds were crusty, but a godsend compared with the cramped quarters downstairs. Kira took the top bunk, where she made herself comfortable, then leant over and pulled an upside-down face at Red.

"Don't you think travel without music's like tobacco without hash?"

"The only thing you'll find on board is a banjo player, and he'll want paying."

I laughed and lifted the covers from my face.

"I doubt we could even afford that at this moment in time."

Cameron, still standing, opened a new pack of cigarettes, and offered them round. I declined his offer, pulled the covers back over my head and went to sleep.

I dreamed I was back in Cameron's treehouse, only this time night had descended and the views were of paramount beauty. Like a giant telescope, the treehouse took me closer than ever to the skies of Asia, presenting portraits that could only be purchased from the Almighty himself. Suddenly I awoke, as the boat docked with a thud. The chill in the air indicated cooler weather, and the commotion below sounded like trouble. I could hear pigs squealing and wings flapping. Startled, I jumped up.

"What's going on?"

"Military," Cameron replied. "They're on the rampage for free goods and people without papers. Probably gonna take the real piss, now that law and order have gone up the spout."

"They were helping themselves to stuff when I was in the hospital." Red had found one of his tablets and swirled it around with some flat fizzy. "Still, at least the riots have finished." He swallowed.

As his voice trailed off, the jingle of brass-type buckles sounded louder and closer. Suddenly two guys in green army fatigues opened our door.

"Documento…!"

Kira started to hand me my passport, but the officer took it before I could grab it. We had to wait until we were checked, stamped, and searched. They took my wallet, turned it inside out and found the hundred dollars I had left.

"Come on man, be a sport." Cameroon moaned, "these girls have gotta get home and as you can see, my friend is injured."

Amusement and anger flushed over their faces. Since they could see that we had nothing else of value and that our passports were in date, they handed me the money and moved off.

"We're lucky." Cameroon sighed, "come on, let's get going."

Possessions ransacked, the natives had thinned out, leaving just a queue of foreigners standing amongst the rubbish while they awaited clearance.

Emelio was among the few caught out. He yelled to Muzz, signalling for smokes, but was out of sight within seconds.

Chasing after him, Muzz disappeared.

"Poor bastard – his papers must have run out!" Red turned to Cameron and shook his head. "They could make him wait weeks if they want to."

"Nah," said Cameron, "Muzz'll drive em mad, they'll both be back in Sweden before you know it!"

A loud squealing suddenly interrupted our musing. Having confiscated one of the peasants' pigs, the military were dragging it away and cracking jokes after it. Halfway down the steps Cameron stopped.

"I bet my bollocks it's on a spit by midnight!"

"Do you really not need 'em?" Red joked. Cameron grinned. "Actually, my friend, I think I do, also a drink."

"I'll second that." Booze sounded good to me as I shivered into the night.

The nearest bar was crammed with thirsty foreigners. We pushed our way to the front, and grabbed a beer and brandy each. Everyone was really restless, so when one of the Yanks took over the table, he quickly monopolised the place. His jokes were sick and sordid but his ability to rip the piss out of folk and make them laugh at themselves kept him in beer all night. It was also a good night for the local hostels, which housed many a tired mind till sunup.

The chance of a mid-morning flight back to Hong Kong made me smile. Manila wasn't a good place to be at the best of times. Red's decision to stay was cool. He had to return to the hospital for check-ups that Cameron offered to assist him with. He directed us to the airport and we waved them off.

There were no shops or food at the airport – it was bare and boring. I could see our plane purring beneath the heat waves outside but the military held the short queue up while they tried a new way of squeezing folks, 'Airport tax'. Since the demotion of Imelda Marcos it seemed that everyone was trying to cash in. We watched them take what they could from the queuing passengers. We ourselves didn't actually have any money for them to take, so after a drawn-out debate, they gave in and let us return to Hong Kong.

There were thousands of bedsits in the city, all with as many problems as the next, so it was easier to head for Anna's in the hope of an IOU. A hard-headed woman she knew we made money, and wanted a piece of it. She gave us twenty-four hours grace and tried to add extra charges for the luggage we had stashed in her cupboards. Seeing it wasn't going to wash, she gave it up as a bad job joke and threw the key to us. I'd only had a few hours kip when she began to bang and chant Chinese and muddled English through the door.

"You get work today, huh. Money make Ming happy."

"You can't expect people to get it up and on at this time!" Kira retaliated.

"Never mind the rats, she's a fucking bloodsucker!"

"Leech more like..." Kira got up and put her ear to the door. "She may be small, but she sounds like an elephant storming off."

Kira winked at me, opened up the door and sneaked into the hall. I knew she was on the razzle for a smoke. While she searched I tried to remove my jeans. Wet patches of pus had seeped out and stuck the denim to my skin. I counted to three and tore them off, it was horrible. Seeing the sores made me feel sick. I covered them with the old baggies of Fin's that I still had, and sneaked down the hall and into the streets where I began to walk, hoping to find a pharmacist and some kind of Chinese cure.

Heroin whispered from every known haunt, and I felt anything but easy, trying to ignore the urges and temptations. I pushed on to the shopping mall where I discovered a shop stocked with multi-purpose medicines. As I entered, a strange sight and smell hit me. A range of unfortunate creatures that had been killed in the name of medicine had been crammed into jars and bottles, their enlarged eyes projecting icy stares from behind the glass. From somewhere out back, an old woman brought the smell of salt and incense with her alongside a jar of marble-type balls that she was carrying. She put it down on the counter and smiled. I rolled the baggies down to show her the problem eating away at me. She shuffled along her shelves and took out a small ladder; climbing two of the steps she offered me what I can only describe as dried bat wings which I declined with a disgusted expression on my face. Changing to plan B, she packed up several tablets and handed them to me, clearing her throat she spoke for the first time.

"Increases speed of healing."

I didn't want to ask what they were made of, just dared myself to try one. Outside, I swallowed one, headed back and waited for it to work. I made it up the stairs and was halfway down the hallway when Anna caught me up, giving me the third degree she burned my ears.

"You go shop but not pay me!"

"For God's sake, Anna, you've got our passports, what is your problem?"

I lost my rag with her a bit – she was so hyper, pushy, and mean. I had never seen her go shopping, or wear anything but the blue and red dresses she alternated. She was being greedy, and impatient. Thankfully, her phone buzzed, which gave me the diversion I needed to escape both her and the ensuing argument.

I found Kira with Puk. Back from India, he had good shit with him. There was a new face too. Nita was from South America, had enough wrinkles to set up shop, and a personality that I didn't quite get to grips with. Her dark hair and baggy eyes brought her hog-like face to life. She seemed half-sensible till she told us she might be pregnant and didn't know who the father was. Raising my eyebrows I took on the joint.

"So where in South America you from?" I finally asked.

"Honduras."

Kira had this laugh that kept escaping without explanation. After Nita had left the room, she let rip.

"Never mind Nita – more like the Honduras hog!"

Puk choked on the banter, while smoke gushed through his nose.

"That's harsh!" he groaned. "But pretty accurate!"

We were in the middle of a laughing fit when Anna stole our buzz. She kept banging on the door which drove us all mad. We knew she wasn't going to give it up so we told her we were getting ready to go.

Selling your soul when sober was anything but easy. Kira, having had a row with her ex-employer, joined me at 'China City. Sassy sent us both to the 'Shangri-La' on a joint venture. I didn't mind the hotel it was just some of the inhabitants and expectations I couldn't stomach. Still giggling over the Honduras hog, we searched the coffee lounge for our client.

"Over there," I said, pointing and laughing quietly.

"Nah, too thin," Kira said.

"What about that one?" Pointing to a small man with a wizard beard I raised Kira's chin, as she saw him she spat lemonade through her nose. Before she could subdue her laughter, I found another possibility.

"How about Harry the hamster?"

We were laughing so much that a few of the hotel residents had started to look over their newspapers and coffee cups.

"Oh-oh, I think we've been spotted."

Kira dried her chin, leaned towards me and pointed ahead. A tallish guy was putting his newspaper away and closed in on us. He spoke, reaching for a hand from each of us.

"I'm Hung."

"Umm …" I laughed. "I'm Sung and this is Lung."

He gave me a strange look. I don't think he had a clue that we were actually taking the piss. He gestured for us to join him at his table, we obliged and sat down. While the waiter danced to the tune of his orders I struggled to keep a straight face. We just wanted to crack up and leave. Listening to him brag about himself and his achievements was hard work, but I knew if I glanced just once at Kira I would have given it up as a bad joke and burst at the seams. A combination of being stoned, alive, and secretly unwilling had really stirred us both up. Two coffees and a beer later, we were heading towards the New Territories. We stopped outside a block of posh apartments and followed him inside. The master bedroom with all its luxuries did nothing for our enthusiasm. The truth was that neither of us could really be bothered, and had wanted out the moment he had paid us. We could hear the shower gushing and knew we had a few minutes to find a way out. Falling onto the bed, we burst into laughter; the hash had hit us hard and we were still giggling. Once the taps had stopped running, we pulled the covers over us and tried to hide.

"What's the plan?" I sniggered.

"Just keep your kit on."

"And that's your answer, is it?"

"Unless you got a better one, yeah. Shit, he's coming!"

Hearing him enter the room we struggled to be quiet. He didn't know we were still dressed till he started to fumble around. Receiving no joy my end, he tried the other... it was a bad game of pass the butt. Every time he touched my middle, it tickled, making me laugh more than ever. Realising that neither of us was going to give in, he sat bolt upright.

"You're like two spring chickens that died before they got stuffed."

Almost suffocating on the feather pillows, we heard him get up, a few seconds later the door slammed and we let rip. Remembering Paulo on the island we nearly choked and died of duck down. Eventually giving it up, we got up.

We found Hung sitting in the lounge. His arms were crossed and his lips were tight with temper. We paused to apologise, but just began to laugh again so we headed back into town where the laughter turned to tears.

After we had ordered hot drinks in the café below Anna's, we simply cried. Heroin had left its damage and I felt like a broken shell needing something to seal up the sides. The froth on my hot chocolate reminded me of melted heroin and the money to spare in my pocket began to talk. We taunted each other with dares, ifs, and maybes. It was ridiculous. I was ready to burst with frustration when Ness came through the door.

Screaming with delight, she settled down next to us and began to offload the latest earner. She had met some Chinese folk who paid well for the delivery of gold. By the time she'd finished, I was wriggling on my chair. The thought of plugging the gold for two hours wasn't that appealing, however, the gear she had on her was. Upstairs, Ness got straight to work. I knew she did gear just not that she had switched from nose to needle again. The fact I no longer used the needle kind of justified the fact that I was doing the gear at all. Ness didn't even know that we had been away. That's how the junkie world is. Most of the time, time is timeless. Once we were numb, life had a whole new meaning. It was one weakness none of us could control.

Kira's presence in 'China City' eased the boring chitchat and put a little entertainment into the conversations. With my legs fast healing, I was able to ditch the tights and expose them without too much interrogation. Mosquito scars were definitely better than needle tracks. For a while time trundled along without any real meaning at all, that was until I woke up face to face with one of the rats again. It scared the shit out of me more than my first encounter with one. Apartments were costly, but when one became available on the eighth floor in a building two blocks down from Anna's, I wasted no time asking the club to loan me the money, which, to my surprise, they did. Eddie Wong counted the cash out on the table before handing over the huge wad. Leaving the club was a pleasure for once. Having gained another habit, I hadn't seen Puk or anyone else for some time. I was feeling good about the apartment, and knocked at his door, on entering, I found Nita skinning-up.

She wasn't pregnant after all and had decided to devote all her time to drugs instead. I had always known she wasn't the full ticket, I also knew that Puk was cashing in on her stupidity. That aside, he'd always made me laugh and I enjoyed his company. I gave him the new address and went and got Kira. Walking out of Anna's felt fab, at last there was one kind of rat I no longer had to sleep with.

Even though the views were only of concrete, Kira loved the apartment. I dumped my stuff down and it felt great – almost normal. Below, a new layout of people littered and decorated the streets. It didn't take long to familiarise myself with the peasants and pushers who were more than willing to deliver just about anything to my door for a small fee. I had no idea how much gear I was doing only that it was too much when measured by the monetary price of street drugs.

Funded by the greedy, and justified by the food it enabled families to purchase from pushing, the city was an ocean of corruption. The stuff poured in from the mainland, and with it came other evils like the dreaded Mandrax a mind-blowing, boggling upper that fucked you up fast. They were highly addictive, and within no time, we were all eating them like *Smarties*. Taking them made us crazy city clubbers who were here, there, and everywhere. They had many effects. Puk fell in the road once and smashed his legs up. Instead of feeling the pain, he just laughed and ran off. Nita got loud. In fact, she got so bad that we sometimes pretended we didn't know her. Puk spent more and more time at the apartment in order to avoid her. She had a nasty habit of lecturing him, or whoever was around, on the dangers of drugs. The fact that she did everything going herself made her a hypocrite and did nothing but cause unwanted arguments.

One of the locals, called Frankie, had just dropped me a gram of heroin when the doorbell went. Puk went to open it.

"You up for this or not…?"

I knew by the expression on his face that it was Nita, but we had to open up to let Frankie out. I let her in and opened a beer. Things were cool till she popped her first pill and asked me to get her a job in the club. Kira gave me a shifty look. We all knew they wouldn't take her, not even if she was the last woman on the planet. Trying to let her down gently was like getting a bear to use a toilet.

"You think I can't do it, right?" She said to me.

"It isn't like that, it's … complicated."

Puk tried to put his arm round Nita in a bid to calm her, but she pushed him aside and began to lash out like an octopus. She caught Puk on the lower lip, splitting it in two places, and threw a punch that broke my nose. Twisting her arm behind her back, Puk and Kira marched her downstairs. By the time I reached the bottom of the stairs, she was storming away, spitting and cussing everyone in her path. Puk said there was nothing doctors could do for a broken nose, and that I'd have to increase the morphine till the pain eased off. He raided the fridge for ice, and put a cold pack on my forehead. It felt horrible at first, but soon helped to ease the pain. Kira crushed up, and placed a long line of pain relief before me. Using my good nostril, I snorted the heroin and slept.

It was around midday that Puk returned and woke me. Apparently Nita had pissed off Anna so much that she had told her to pack up and get out.

"Where did she go?"

"Singapore, I think."

Sitting up, my face still felt sore.

"Goodbye and good riddance I say!"

My decision to go to work early was merely to change the scene, get out and that. The few girls there were too busy powdering their faces for any kind of conversation, so I opened a bottle of Regal in a bid to drown my drug depression. Most of them were cool, but there's always one wanting to score points with the boss. Seeing the Bessie Bunter look-alike come clattering towards me I knew she was going to be trouble before she spoke.

"You can't open that without permission!"

"Stick it on my bill."

"You must put it back."

"Belt up and bog off, will ya?"

She turned and shuffled towards the entrance with an invisible spoon which she was soon to turn into a whisk. Several minutes later, a bouncer wearing a pinstripe suit, strolled my way.

"You should be drinking with clients."

"And you should get a better life! If you're so bothered, go fuck 'em yourself."

"This is no good, Sharm."

"What is then, come on, tell me." I pointed to a crowd of people entering. "You, them, come on, I wanna know!"

I waved my glass of Regal as though it were a fist and found myself walking steadily towards him. He backed off and went straight towards the office. Eddie Wong rarely left his headquarters for anything other than sex or money, so I was surprised when he approached me. In his office he pushed a luxury leather chair my way and poured more Regal…

"Let's have it. You didn't come in last night or the one before." Slowly he drank.

I chewed on the question while he topped me up. I couldn't tell him about the drugs, or how out of control my life was. Besides, I still owed him a shitload of money so I told him there was a problem in England.

"We can't afford bad publicity or ripples in the water, there's too much at stake." Seeing my tears, his voice softened. "Take the night off, start again tomorrow."

He got up and opened the door, but bad news was brewing outside as he did so. Armed police had sealed the exits off while queues of glamorous girls waited impatiently for their papers to be checked. I had nothing to worry about from the department of Immigration, unlike some who shuffled nervously.

"Routine, right…?" I turned to Eddie.

"More a pain in the – how you say – aasss!"

"So much for good publicity, aye…"

Knowing I wouldn't be leaving for some time, I sat in the lobby. The girls were put into national categories. The Hong Kong girls appeared irritated by the interruption and cussed accordingly. The Chinese won by a long shot. The queue for their lot trailed right across the dance floor and disappeared into the changing rooms. Thais only made it as far as the executive lounge, and the Cambodians just made it past the bandstand. After that, I couldn't recognise where they were from, so I gave up guessing and left them in the 'stranger' section. Two hours later, the police left the club with a handful of girls, and a bouncer who had something he shouldn't. One of the girls cried so hard she left a damp floor behind her.

Once I'd been stamped and given the nod to leave, I went somewhere I hadn't been for quite some time and was surprised to see Fran still hard at work in the Taverna. She poured me a drink and wanted to know all about the islands and where Red was which was anyone's guess. After three beers, I told the whole story, which was just as well because the DJ kept getting louder and louder. Just as I was about to leave, I found myself face to face with Jimmie and his famous smile. He tried to chat, but it was hard to hear anything with the Queen of Pop playing, so we left everyone to get into the groove.

The park was relatively bare due to the change in season, but there was enough cover left under which we could skin-up. We chatted for ages about drugs and stuff. For a moment, I thought he was going to apologise for introducing me to Red and cocaine. Instead, he put an arm round me that was hard to refuse. The warmth of his body was welcoming, and for a moment, all my troubles disappeared. He lit a second smoke and began to preach. Most of it was sensible stuff and kind of confirmed his unspoken apology. He told me about a doctor who could prescribe tablets to help wean me off it. He wrote the name down on a slip of paper and put it in my pocket.

Comfortable in his arms, I nodded. I didn't want to end up like the old-timers wasting away, waiting for the city to finish them off. But some days it felt like there was no escaping heroin. Getting off it would be one thing, but regaining all the self-worth I'd lost was going to be hard. I mean, wasn't that why I was still on it? Because the damn stuff had nagged me to death till I gave into it and all its lowlife ways. It hadn't really occurred to me that there was help in the city for people like me, people who were lost, misunderstood, numb, and pretty useless most of the time. My whole world had become so reliant on heroin that I rarely thought of much else.

The apartment was empty when I finally returned to it. There was just a note inviting me to some party across town, but I couldn't be bothered. I didn't sleep much, just whirled the conversation I'd had with Jimmie around my head. The next day I examined the doctor's name and address. I called a cab and went to see what Jimmie had been on about. Inside the building sat all sorts who bore the markings of heroin. After thirty minutes, the doctor saw me and prescribed a small bottle of pink tablets to be taken orally as and when required. I promised myself I would try them, and lit a cigarette. And that's another thing, I thought, you smoke too much.

Bad Luck

I saw police driving away from the club as I left my cab. On entering two more left the lift. Their green khaki trousers and matching tops still looked ruffled from whatever had happened. There had been commotion going on everywhere for weeks, but the mess upstairs was the most disruptive yet.

Inside, tables and chairs were overturned, glass littered the floor, and the smell of Regal filled the tiled entrance. Some of the girls were helping to clear up. As I approached, I could see spots of blood amongst the broken glass. One of the girls told me that Kira had had a row over pay. It was something the club did every month depending on the amount of Regal purchased and drunk at the table by the punters. It was a perk, a bonus, whatever you want to call alcohol purchase and poisoning. They had tried to undercut her and, when she tried to prove her point, a heated debate had got out of hand. The bouncers had stepped in to restrain her and another girl, all of which had led to an explosion. Apparently Kira had thrown a glass ashtray at them which shattered, after that a table and so on.

I knew Mandrax would be responsible because no one lost it that way unless they were screwed on pills. I hadn't seen Kira for a few days, consumed by drugs we were all, all over the place. Unable to deal with the situation, I walked straight back out. They'd be looking to me for some kind of logical explanation, and I just didn't have one. I chain-smoked downstairs before hailing a cab to take me to the local nick. At first, they wouldn't allow me to see Kira, but a second officer offered me five minutes. I could hear Kira shouting as I followed him up the stairs. Handcuffed, and sat on a chair centre of the room her lip was bleeding. As I entered she hurled abuse at the officers in the room and behind me. One gave her a right hander across the face and several more till she shut up. I tried to talk some sense into both parties only wanting them to stop the hitting. A packet of cigarettes and I put one in Kira's mouth, backing up the officers stopped and let me light it. Removing it every few minutes it didn't take her long to drain it down to the butt. Red blotches and scratches covered her arms and legs. Her silk shorts were torn from the fight, and her feet were bare. Not knowing what to say, I simply asked her where she'd been.

"Party across town, I was tired when I got back. Knew I shouldn't have gone in tonight. It wouldn't have got to this if the bloody club could count bottles. Before I know it this lot turned up. Roughed me right up they have. Can you get me a drink?"

In pain she blew hard on her cheeks. Scrutinizing me the officers watched as I walked towards a ceramic sink, filled a cup and held it up for her. The cuffs were cutting into her wrists, so I asked the officer to loosen them, but he didn't give a shit. Holding a second fag to her mouth several times, I tried to ease the cold turkey I saw emerging. The flaps on her shorts shook as she shivered. Knowing they were about to show me the door, I remembered the pink pills I had. I'd just unscrewed the top when the officer by the door wrenched my hand behind my back sending the tablets all over the floor. Reading the label on the bottle, a second officer smiled.

"You're under arrest for trafficking in a police station."

At first it just didn't sink in. The pills had been prescribed by a professional person and I hadn't even tried one. Expecting them to give them back to me, I pulled one of my arms free and reached for the bottle, but the officers weren't letting up and forced the cuffs on me.

"Leave her alone, you fucking idiots!" Kira repeatedly yelled but the more she did so the more they belted her from head to foot. I couldn't look as they punched her face and body. I screamed for them to stop, but they just marched me away.

I was shocked, devastated, and a bit broken, and for a while even the thought of withdrawal didn't bother me. I missed Fran's company, Kira's chat, and Jimmie's jokes that usually ended with one of his warm bear hugs. Eventually I drifted heavily away in the hope I'd wake up in heaven. Instead, a female officer exercising a baton on the bars blew my tender ears.

"How are you feeling?"

Not sure if she meant me or not, I didn't move. Then she said it again. Sitting up, I spoke.

"Like shit!"

My limbs were limp like a bundle of string, prickly heat returning my anxieties were pumping their fuels round my system. Only the start of it, I shuddered…

"Up, up!"

She opened the door and gestured for me to follow her. This unexpected concern indicated that I wasn't going anywhere for a while. A cold sweat on my skin it was hell. I followed her to the hall where she told me to sit down.

"Doctors here are no good." She returned with some thin chains which she wrapped around my waist before leading me to a wagon where two other sick prisoners waited. Their long-distance stares achieved only from too many drugs bored into the metal side-panels of the wagon. I didn't speak Cantonese, so they just nodded every now and then in junkie recognition.

The police officer drove without a care for anything in front of him – or behind him, for that matter. Ten minutes later, we halted abruptly. Outside, we were directed to some concrete steps. Climbing to the top of them was hard work. We puffed and panted; finally at the top we turned left and into a hallway. Two doors down, we entered a room. It was bare except for an impressive bottle of green liquid. The officers released the cuffs from all three of us, and nodded towards the cups. The other wasted no time pouring and guzzling till their cheeks became flushed and their faces relaxed. Smoking without a care in the world the officers didn't give a damn. The situation was shit. On the one hand, I was getting done for trafficking. On the other, I was being given the chance to legally overdose on as much methadone as I could stomach.

The liquid was thick and treacle-like, as I struggled to get it down, I began to sip my sorrows away, and to ensure the death of withdrawal I downed a second lot. It was strong stuff, and took effect almost immediately. Injections of strength ran down my legs, and my fingers began to find a normal wiggle. Pimples shrank, and bones hinged back together. It really was quite magical making its permanent elimination all the harder to comprehend.

Walking or should I say staggering back down the stairs was a struggle. My companions swayed and tripped some of the way, occasionally breaking their fall against me. My internal heaters were alight, but the only problem was that I now couldn't turn them down. By the time I reached the police van, I was seeing through glazed eyes, my body was so hot I'm surprised it didn't self-combust. The movement of the vehicle made us feel worse, so much so that one of the others began to vomit all over the floor. The officer who sat next to me placed a boot on his head and kept him down in his own mess. Watching the guy moan and splutter was cruel and twisted, but I don't think the police cared whether their prisoners lived or died. Oblivious to his pleas and illness, they kept him down all the way back to the station.

By the time we had returned, the guy had passed out, and needed to be carried to his cell. I was hot, and to say I was numb would be an understatement. They could have amputated a limb and I wouldn't have known. My guts churned like the ocean, and my cell became a sea of vomit. Desperate for the sickness to subside I lay very still. I found myself in a desert of heroin, on a horse with no name. The tune repeated itself over and over again until I disappeared. A day later I awoke feeling like death. I had half- expected to see Kira next to me at some point. I stared down the rows of cells searching for her, but there was nobody, just the guys from before who now looked like a couple of grim reapers in need of a top-up. With the cold gnawing at me, I called for someone to come.

"What about court, and what about another visit for methadone?"

"Too late, much too late..."

They were playing cruel mind games that only a small mind would be satisfied with. The food that arrived made me feel queasy, so I passed it to the guys next door. It was six in the morning when they returned to take us to court. As I had hoped, they removed the chains before taking me into the dock. Dressed only in Chinese satin, I felt cold and stupid. Luckily I'd taken my jacket to the club that night and still had it. Fran's and Kira's presence lifted my spirits slightly but the bruising on Kira's face had darkened and appeared patchy, mind boggled I couldn't think straight. All I knew was that I'd do anything to get out and dry up all the pain that was clinging to me. The judge was English, as were most of them.

He adjourned the case and granted bail on the condition that I surrender my passport and sign on at the police station every night. Waiting for the girls to fetch my passport was torture. I was so sick I could hardly think, let alone move. An hour later, I was outside where I gulped relief and freedom with Fran and Kira. Kira, cussing the police and club, spat fireworks all the way across town until the words were stuck in my mind like a broken record. Eventually, she ran out of stuff to say, and the silence was bliss.

Our cab dropped us off at the end of our notorious street. Seething with anger at my situation, I nodded to everyone who'd something to sell. No sooner had I opened the door and dug out some cash, than the goods began to arrive, heroin, hash, and pills.

Feeling Blue

With the passage of time marked by takeaway grub and powdered puddings the day dragged miserably. I felt tired, but my energies were running far too high for sleep. I smoked pack after pack of Camels until the time hit ten, forcing me up to sign on at the local station.

Of course, the police thought it was a joke and loved every minute of the mess they'd made. They pretended they couldn't find the paperwork for ages and made no secret of their amusement while searching for it. Thirty minutes later they were ready for me to sign. Pissed off with everything I went home and slept on the settee.

It was the throbbing in my ears that woke me. Pounding at the irritation, my fingers became electric drills that would enter my skull if I didn't find a diversion. I forced myself up and out, and strolled toward 'Taverna' where I made myself socialize with the rest of the junkie world. Inside Ness and Jimmie were sitting around a new table, gassing to a weirdo I hadn't seen before they spun it, while Kira helped herself to drinks from behind the bar. I sat down and joined the so-called circle of friends and listened. The latest gossip, apart from my own fate, was the gold- running Ness had mentioned before.

I watched Puk pour his beer into a toby jug. It was something he often did, on the basis that it tasted better.

When he was finished pouring, he shoved the newcomer up and introduced me.

"This is Minky – better known as Metal Mink. He'll be our lead and diversion. See, everyone will think he's the courier and be watching him like a hawk, which takes the flak off us, beautiful huh?"

Mink looked like a cross between a Rottweiler and a posh Poodle. You didn't have to be Einstein to see he was gay. He moved like a woman and spoke with enough femininity to pull anyone who sought his services. The red hair, high heels, and blue eye shadow made him – or her – look pretty scary.

"It's more than a job," Mink whispered to me, "it's a three-month butt break."

His comment failed to bring on the bout of laughter it normally would. Getting up I paused, "whatever turns you on..."

"Oh, but the gold does, baby."

Mink put five fags down, and spun the new table, which stopped at Ness. She took one of the cigarettes and looked up at me.

"Don't fancy it then? Boss needs one more on this trip and four the next time round. We leave tonight, it's all arranged. Just think about the next one. Beats clubbing any day..."

Depressed I got up to go but Jimmie grabbed my hand and pulled me back.

"C'mon, we know its shit what happened, but it'll be okay

– you'll see. Try this lawyer. He's English and damn good." Jimmie took a pen from his pocket and began to write. "Use 'Tow' hairdressers to find the building. From there, J C's two down and three up."

Feeling shackled, I made for the toilet, where I crushed and snorted heroin. Since I didn't want to celebrate tomorrow's arse runners, and really wasn't sure if I'd do it anyway, I took the fire exit out back and made my way to the hairdressers. There, motionless and moodless, I watched the transformation of hair through tinted glass windows. On one half of the shop, they were cutting bobs as though they were going out of fashion while on the other side the oldies were having their blue rinses. The loud dryers reminded me of the airport terminal. I walked two blocks down and prepared to go three up. Just as Jimmie had told me, it was there that I found the initials J C displayed in brass letters. I went over the J a few times before pushing the door ajar. Behind the door a full head of brown hair was heavily buried in a file. Below the desk, a pair of leather shoes tapped the ground impatiently. Sensing someone in the room the lawyer put the file down and stood up. Nice looking guy, there was a lot of compassion in his face.

"I didn't know I had any current appointments?"

"You don't, can I stay?"

Resuming his seat he pushed the chair opposite forward with his shoe and closed the file. Raising his eyebrows he was all ears. I didn't really know where to start, but his patience helped me put things into perspective.

After a shower of tears, two teas, and a much-needed heart-to-heart, I was on the road to reassurance. He told me his fee, payable in instalments prior to the case. He wasn't cheap, but because he was the only structural figure in my life, I agreed. Downstairs I was surprised to see Kira waiting for me.

"Thought I'd meet you, fancy something sweet before heading home?"

"Okay, lead the way."

We walked to the ice cream parlour across town. Over two rounds of vanilla, we discussed everything that had happened. Afterwards, we went to see what the Chinese market was all about. Like a train it snaked along the back streets, its carriages full of exotic goods. Candles, trinkets and cup holders were just a few of the delights we encountered. We stopped at a hat stall where we tried several on for a laugh, looking up I saw silks that captivated me. I pulled two down, took the best of them and bought it. Moving onwards, we rummaged through a box of lippy holders. I had just found one I liked when Kira gave me a tug and a nod.

"Well, well, well, look what the cat dragged in!"

I looked up to see Red. Topped with a large straw hat it overshadowed some of the tell-tale sighs an addict carries. He wasn't looking in our direction. His arm hung loose from a grey T-shirt, and the weight he'd gained filled a pair of sky-blue jeans. In one hand he held a pair of designer glasses, in the other, some money he was shaking above his head.

"Hasn't changed then…!" Kira laughed.

"Come on, let's sneak up on him."

I pulled Kira with me as I pushed myself through a small crowd I watched him haggle a further minute before moving in.

"Just pay the old girl, you tight git!"

I saw the Cheshire grin spread before he had even seen us.

"Girls, how's it going?"

For a moment it felt good, and I was pleased to see him.

"Arm's good again then?" I asked.

"Yeah, the 'ospital in Manila finished it off nicely. Company was good too."

Hugging us did nothing to calm his haggling retailer, the Chinese woman merely got louder and louder. I pulled away from him and stood straight.

"You better pay her before she blows a fuse." Knowing anything was better than nothing, the woman let him have the shades half-price and shooed him on his way. It was just like old times, only we didn't use the park, we went straight to the apartment.

Red stood in the doorway admiring the place.

"Wow, you did it then? No more rats, huh?" Red approached the couch and got comfortable.

"Listen, I'm only back for a week. Any chance of, you know," pleading, he patted the couch and wiggled his eyebrows.

I didn't really have a problem with it. Besides, the extra company would be good. So I gave in.

"So, what you really doing here?" I asked.

"Collecting some clothes then going straight. I've had enough."

"You don't go straight for one week! What, no more Thailand?"

"Actually no, they're bringing in new death laws. Foreigners will probably be the first to feel it. I'm going to find something else to do."

The more he tried to convince us the more we laughed. Kira got up and flicked the kettle on, poking her head round the door, she zoomed in on Red.

"There's a job going in the club, or maybe Metal Mink could help."

Red sat up, raising his left eyebrow.

"Who the fuck is he when he's at 'ome?"

"Some freak with gold fever," I added.

The description of Metal Mink and all that went with him took us well into the evening. That's when I had to get serious. Leaving Kira to tell Red all the bad news, I arranged to meet them later and headed into town for work. As I arrived at the club, I passed by the payments office. Outside it stood several muma sans, knowing I'd never be heard over the gaggle of geese I left my pay for later. Sassy called to me as she saw me pass. Eddie had been giving her a hard time over what had happened, and wanted everybody to keep better time. I assured her that everything was cool and left her to her conversation. She didn't need to know about the curfew, she already knew enough. Seated at a busy table, the atmosphere was anything but mellow, I was dreading ten o'clock. It was around that time that punters got pissed, slurred their speech, and threw money to the wind in the name of want.

I couldn't concentrate or take in any of the usual crap. Searching for a way out of the shit I was in, I let the other girls at the table do all the talking. I heard one of them say Madonna would be coming to Hong Kong after the making of *Shanghai Surprise*. While I digested this energising thought, my eyes followed a Chinese girl to the dance floor. Her hair flowed in sync with her silk dress, and for a few minutes, I was lost in her elegance. But as ten o'clock approached, I became anxious, irritable and tense, it was time to go. My life had become a vicious circle of events I could do nothing about, even the thought of maybe seeing Madonna made no difference to how I was feeling. Eventually, I got up and just walked out in the hope that I wouldn't be missed. As I left, I passed the executive lounge, Honey was inside, like the fixtures and fittings she would be there forever.

On my return, Sassy went mad, probing my brain for answers. She told me that the whole table had gone into confusion after I had left; not letting up from her interrogation she went on and on. I wanted to tell her to stuff it, shove it and do it herself. The fact I'd become nothing more than a Chinese takeaway, hacked me off but, with my case only a month away and escalating debts, I swallowed hard and made up some shit about feeling sick so she assigned me to another table. Watching them rinse themselves with Regal and put the world to rights did my head in. They had nothing to say and said what they had to, too loudly.

This sort of ducking and diving lasted a week before Sassy called me into her office. She knew everything and was relieving me from her employment. I sat down and smirked.

"I see good news travels fast in this city."

"I'm sorry. We told you once before we can't have bad publicity of any kind."

"And selling souls is fucking legal, is it?" Angered by the comment, Sassy didn't answer. "Feeding the fuckers up on alcohol and sex, you're sick!"

Totally pissed off I left her office. Passing the tuck shop several girls in posh silks sat chewing chicken drummers. Wondering what it was about chickens I continued on my way to the locker rooms. After emptying my locker, I went to collect my monthly commission. Due to my heroin habit, I hadn't done a lot of drinking, so the pay was poor. As I left, I saw three new faces awaiting employment. I leant over a plush chair and gave a pair of gloves to one of the girls.

Sassy had also relieved me of my debt as well as my job, so had left me little to moan about. With the rent and my lawyer fees due, I went to see what bright ideas the others might have.

Entering 'Taverna' I saw Red; having called Jimmie up, he was wrestling his healed arm against Jimmie's good one. The table swayed from side to side and rocked as their energies exchanged. Without speaking or taking her eyes from them, Kira passed me a glass of rum and continued to cheer them on. Jimmie took a deep breath and pushed Red's arm flat onto the table, loving the glory he proposed a toast to celebrate his win.

"You're gonna have to work on that, my man!" Jimmie joked.

Red grinned. "Yeah, a few more weeks and I'll knock you dead." He rubbed his wrist before touching my shoulder. "How things…?

"Oh, you know…"

I lit up then told them all about the carry on at the club. Red thought it was great that they had written off the debt and suggested we go have a gamble.

"What, the casino?" I asked.

I took some coins from my bag and fed them to the cigarette machine while I whirled the suggestion around.

"Yeah, man," Red whistled, "you and Kira could clean up over there. Can't believe I didn't think of it sooner. Place is a gold mine."

"Certainly a good night," Jimmie added.

"You not gonna show us where it is then?" Kira asked glancing to Red.

"Nah – got a few faces to see tonight, it's easy." Red said. "Just take the ferry to Macao. They go every hour tonight."

I looked at Kira, and shrugged. It certainly sounded different, and we both needed some cash. Jimmie hadn't seen the apartment, so he came back with us while we changed. After giving us the thumbs up, he went off with Red.

Signing on at the police station first was a pain in the ass, but something that had to be done so we went there first. We then hurried across town to the docking bays. The first queue was full but fortunately there were still seats available on the second. As it cruised across the waves, the craft made me feel giddy. The seats were too tiny to provide any kind of real comfort, so we spent a lot of the journey trying to figure out who the strange and serious looking people fixed to their seats and newspapers were. Speculating was easy, hiding our laughter wasn't.

At the terminus, we got caught up in the confusion of shuffling feet and purring cabs, finally we got dropped at the Casino Royale along with everyone else. Girls in bunny suits, hoping tips would fill their trays, flitted about the eager and desperate folk. Snobs in suits threw money around while others sucked flutes of freebies while gathering the guts to gamble.

We made our way towards the roulette table, where we watched a wealthy woman rule. As her bets continued to arrive, so did her audience. We took a chance, and joined her. Her numbers came home and the excitement grew. We increased our bets and won bigger bucks each time. Then, not wanting to lose it, we took a back seat. The numbers kept coming in and the players roared with satisfaction. Twenty minutes later, destiny changed its course. After one loss, the woman took her chips and cashed up. We were about to leave when a dumpy man in a pinstripe suit approached us and introduced himself as Tally. He called us back to the table where he began to play. He wasn't bothered about losing large sums of money; in fact, he seemed to thrive on the fact that he had it to lose. While he gambled we listened to what he had to say. He was looking for foreign croupiers to take back to Singapore with him. We moved on to the blackjack table where he told us to watch the croupier.

"Good girls are hard to find, and European croups are like gold dust."

I saw a twinkle enter Kira's eyes; it was a great opportunity and one I'd have to pass up on. As the night progressed, he handed us each a business card. Tired and tanked up, I struggled to make head or tail of it.

"Call me," he said. "The work's easy and the money's great. Beats anything here, I'll even throw in the flights."

Heading off to make a phone call, Tally disappeared. Done for, we retired to a hotel and slept well.

The morning had a tranquil feel about it. I emptied my bag and began to count the money we had won.

"What's there?" Kira asked.

"Enough for the rent and a look around here."

While we cured our hangovers with heroin, we could hear the sound of horse's hooves which became louder and louder. We went over to the window and looked down from it. On the street outside our hotel, horse-drawn carriages were queuing for the ongoing customers leaving the hotel. We went down and as I paid the receptionist I enquired what it was all about.

"Everybody loves the island tour. It's all part of the attraction. Get in, go see."

We decided to treat ourselves, so we packed up and hopped inside one of the carriages. The road circling the island was beautiful in itself. A pattern of blue ceramics decorated the outer layer of brickwork. Beyond that, a variety of palms and exotic plants also knew their place. Trotting on, we passed a giant fish fountain whose morning mist was really refreshing. Every few minutes we approached and passed another design. Dragons, dogs and lions all contributed to the monumental scene set before us. Speechless at the scenery, we absorbed it quietly. I think the giant Buddha offering peace to the world won me over. It came as no surprise when Kira told me she wanted to take Tally up on his job offer. Because of my curfew I couldn't go, things hadn't been easy since the club row in fact they were bloody hard and as much as I'd miss her I couldn't stand in her way.

Belly Up

The apartment felt pretty empty after Kira left. And with Red also planning to do one at the end of the week, I was beginning to feel lonely. I scored some heroin from a local haunt in my street. Frankie had been half-healthy when I had first got to know him but as the heroin hooked him, his skin had become yellow and jaundice-like; thin and flaky it barely covered his skeleton. His mind permanently occupied with making money, he rarely washed and smelt really bad. He was in his early twenties, and I knew he wouldn't see thirty. He bagged the white rocks and took my money. I knew he was in need of good food, but there were no prizes for guessing where the cash would end up. Patting his skinny dog, I closed the door.

When I reached the commercial end of my street, I got in a cab and went to register with one of the escort agencies. The office was on the third floor of an old building. Inside, crazy women conversed on telephones. One of them hung up, shook my hand and pulled a form from a metal drawer. I put my name on paper, and work was instantaneous. They sent me to the 'Regent' where I was to meet a local banker or broker named Lin Wah.

He was well-dressed and totally into himself, his work, and his car. I struggled to accommodate him with suitable conversation and ended up building sandcastles with my special fried rice. My mind kept wandering to Singapore. I suppose I was wondering what Kira was up to, what the casino looked like, and whether or not she would bump into Nita. Having drunk myself stupid in 'China City', brandy no longer appealed to me. Lin's self-portrait only increased with his intake. There was nothing he couldn't or wasn't about to do – the worst kind by all accounts. My boredom became obvious from the yawning that followed, that's when he realized I'd had enough and offered to pay for my conversation. A customer of the hotel, his main money was upstairs so that's where we went. I had no intention of doing anything else. I just wanted to go home, wherever that was.

He slammed the door hard, emptied his pockets and grabbed at my waist. I told him to sod off, but it only increased his temper and a fight broke out between us. He clamped his hands around my arms and pinched and pushed me down. I yelled at him, but he just retaliated by shoving and slapping until I was forced onto the bed, his weight and breathing heavy on top of me. My face stung from back of his hand, and my top tore like a paper bag. I yelled really loudly. When he heard a key in the lock, he fast found his feet. As the bellboy entered, Lin made a dash for the door and disappeared.

"Fucking nutter!" I yelled.

The bellboy poured some water and set it before me.

"Bloody iko..."

"You mean psycho."

"Yeah, sicco."

"Psycho, sicco, it's all the same."

I took the glass from him and drank. Waiting for me he wandered around the room checking it out, I suppose.

"This yours..?"

He had opened a drawer and showed me a full wallet. A moment passed between us. We both knew it belonged to the fleeing party, but he insisted I have it. I gave him a large tip and shared the lift to the lobby with him. He insisted that I have a drink before I left and found me a table next to the glass surround. I was pissed at myself for not being able to get off heroin or get anything together. I was lost in a city held together by drugs and disaster, a place where everything was lost unless you were sold or stoned.

On my return to the apartment, I found happiness shining out of Red's face; he was sifting through a pile of cocaine while his fingers fetched and filtered it. I spoke as I got over the surprise and shock.

"I thought you were leaving, going straight, and getting it together?"

"I am – tomorrow night. But, when Thai offered to tick me this … Well, it was all too much."

"And what if he comes 'ere looking for ya? What am I supposed to say?"

"You ain't seen me, have ya! Besides, he don't know you, or that I'm 'ere. You up for it or not, one for the road, aye?"

I stared at the pile of powder. I hadn't touched any

cocaine since the near miss at Brad's that night, but its avalanche was no harsher than the life I was leading. Besides, I could smell and feel it pulling at my system before it had even entered my blood. My mouth began to water and the smell of its toxins captured me once again.

"You know you want it!" Red had that sales look again, the one I should have slapped long ago. I'd been innocent, outnumbered and naive then, now it was pure addiction attacking me.

"You're such an arse! One line, that's it."

"Leave it out it's far too good for that."

The wet spoon indicated he'd already done a hit, and his impatient hands wasted no time getting on with the next. I rolled my shirtsleeve up and prepared my arm for the fix. My veins had healed and stood up in no time. While my internal angels battled for rights, I took a back seat.

I watched Red pierce the skin and push the plastic together, giving me all the syringe had.

"Fuck, I'd forgotten just 'ow good it is."

The rush was soaring to the top of my internal skyscraper and about to eject through the roof when it took a U-turn and forced my special fried rice back up. Just making the bathroom, I let rip. The rush was so short and the price so high, but its hold was indescribable.

"You ready for another?"

Red was an animal around coke. I lifted my head from the toilet to cuss him, but was too preoccupied with emptying the remains of my stomach to do so. No one ever used the bell, so when it rang, I jumped out of my skin and, momentarily, off the white merry-go-round.

"Who the fuck's that?"

"How the hell should I know?"

Red's impatient paranoia irritated me; instead of getting up he just pulled the gear closer to himself and pretended he was invisible. I made my way to the door and stared through the spyhole. It was Ness. She'd had her hair done, and was wearing an expensive sequined dress. I knew she must have seen Fran and wouldn't pass on seeing Red for anything. I opened the door and let her in. Despite my dysfunctional state, she gave me a big hug and ogled the table.

"Umm, yummy, do me one up."

"You not with the others you went with?" Trying to be sociable was painful, so I kept it minimal.

"No news yet; I don't miss Metal Mink. The guy was gross. We got split up after landing. That's when I decided to do one rather than deliver. I thought getting through the city would be the hardest, but it was the open country that proved me wrong."

As he handed Ness a loaded needle, Red's eyes lit up.

"What, you robbed the Nepalese?"

"Sure did."

Opening her bag, Ness displayed a small example of her new fortune.

"You could have been killed!"

"Yeah, but I ain't. I'm here celebrating with you two!"

"Fuck man. I didn't think you had it in yer!"

She took the fix, dropped her dress and went straight into her groin. She was a great-looking girl, but beneath her clothes there were more tracks than a tractor left in winter. Feeling sorry for her I tried not to stare at the appalling and ghastly scars running all over her body. As she clocked my disgust, she smiled.

"It's okay. I know."

"Don't it bother ya?"

"Yeah, but what to do? If I have a habit, I must feed it."

Red pulled the belt round my arm and injected it with another mind-blowing rush, then himself. Coming down from the rush, he managed to muster up a few tacky words.

"So how much did you get for the gold?"

It was so typical of Red. If his greed was to be weighed and measured he would most certainly be very heavy.

Ness stared at him through polluted eyes; her mind now all over the place, she just shrugged.

"Enough to retire on."

Unable to get another in the groin, she began to attack her fingers. I had to look away as the blood trickled down her arm and slowly dried somewhere around her middle. We flew until our wings collapsed and the table was wiped clean. Then we crushed heroin to iron our nerves out. With bionic blood and clogged nostrils Ness clutched her bag and left. I climbed into bed and tried to find some sleep. For once it came relatively easily and I was away in no time. In my dream, I could see Red. Catching a dust cloud he threw powder from it to the people. I was in deep sleep when banging woke me, followed by Red who shook me and shouted.

"Wake up, Sharm. It's the fucking cops!"

I stirred and turned over.

"You gotta get up," he continued.

"What's so important, and why can't you get the door? They got nothing on us. You did clean up, didn't you?"

"'Course I did."

"Then what the hell do they want?"

Instead of opening up, I crushed the last of my heroin and snorted it. I suddenly realised that it was me they'd come for, and froze in my skin. I grabbed the clock on the shelf and shook it. It was five in the morning and I hadn't signed in at the nick. It was now me hitting and yelling at Red.

"What am I gonna do?"

"Answer the bloody door before they kick it in for a start."

I could hear the police begin to bash it down. Rushing to it, I fell on the table and cut my leg, but that was the least of my worries. With their weight on the door, it was a struggle to undo it. Instead of helping, Red just stood there looking stupid. As the door gave, I went flying. Before I could stand or speak, they had cuffed me.

"What did you throw out there?"

They repeated the question over and over again, while they

squeezed my wrists for an answer. When Red refused to face me I shouted at him gaining a few seconds of his attention. Like an injured bird, his eyes flitted around the apartment; that's when I knew he was stitching me up. Only problem was, I was the only one who knew it, and, in my current state of affairs, I really was up shit creek without a paddle. I had no idea exactly what Red had done, but my intuition told me that it wasn't good. Within minutes Bob Dylan, Steely Dan, Prince, and the police, like my clothes, were nothing but a tangled mess on the apartment floor. Feathers from the mattress and powders from the cleaning bottles made me sneeze. In their temper the police threw the stuff everywhere including the walls; they tore down shelves, emptied drawers and deliberately trod photos of the island into the floor. It was in those pictures that I lost myself.

The presence of two new officers broke my trance. Stamping on the floor with his Doc Martins, the first muttered harsh words; a few seconds later the second officer began to shout in Chinese. Seeing that I had switched off, the first of the two officers tightened his harness and opened the window. He placed one foot carefully in front of the other, then clipped his ropes to a pole and called for the other officer. Once they were out of sight, there was nothing to do but wait.

While they retrieved whatever it was, hurt and hatred surged through me as the drugs had earlier – eventually leading to tears of frustration.

"How could ya?"

With boiling blood I turned to Red, who was standing motionless, staring at the wall; I think he thought that if he looked there long enough it would swallow him or something. Another officer then entered the apartment and began to sound off.

"It would save us a lot of bother if you just told us what we were looking for."

"Well, tell them," I said to Red.

Everyone turned to him, and, for a second, I felt I was winning. When he didn't answer, the new officer shoved me hard into the settee and stormed outside. Minutes later, two officers appeared with a brown paper package. My internal organs momentarily melted into disbelief and despair. I knew if he didn't play ball, I was bang to rights.

Downstairs a crowd had congregated at the front of it, with their cameras, stood the press. As they saw them starting to click at us, the police covered our faces and rushed toward the waiting police wagons. The journey was short. I had spent enough weeks visiting the place night after night, and for what, being a gullible fool. Kira was sunning it up, and Red was selling his way out faster than fast. Unable to look at him I leaned my chin on my left shoulder and closed my eyes. Having just arrested a whole gang of pissheads the station stank of beer and BO. We passed some of them as we were marched upstairs. The police cleared the table of paperwork and sat us either side of it. A moment of emptiness followed before a female head honcho entered. I asked for my lawyer but she refused. She placed documentation in front of us both, folded her arms and stood back.

"Okay, let's start talking! This," waving a hand in the air, she pointed to Red, "is obviously your boyfriend."

The mere thought revolted me. I'd never even kissed him. I moved my wrists in the cuffs, and tried to neutralize the statement.

"And this," she continued, "is a whole lot of heroin."

I forced myself to look at Red, but he had only one thing in mind – himself.

"Look man, why would I risk all this? My girl lives in Manila, and well, she's pregnant."

"You did well with one arm, didn't you?" I screamed.

He continued to babble and I had to listen to him tell them all about Manila and his life there. The officer in charge was about to wave his story to one side when he produced a ticket from his back pocket. The departure date was for the following day. He might as well have taken a hammer and just battered me with it.

At least the bruising would eventually go. This would last forever. Knowing I was beaten, I stood up ready to hit the cells, but was forced back down by the bitch from hell. They couldn't be bothered with interviews, fingerprints, or debates they just wanted a signature to wrap it up for the morning. They released my hands and gave me a pen. Because of my innocent mistake previously, I'd become a sitting duck for everyone in the station – including Red.

"Sign it!" she demanded.

I threw the pen with great accuracy, hitting Red hard in the chest.

"You sign it, shithead."

The bitch repeatedly hit out, stinging my face time and time again. I was far too angry to acknowledge the humiliation, instead the desperation on Red's face started to amuse me. His eyes were weak and wild. He hadn't shaved for days, and the stubble now accumulating around his square jaw made him look a lot more than thirty. He had been sweating, and the room was beginning to pong. My face tingled and my heart stung, so when they placed us in separate cells, I was more than happy to fall into the junkie limbo calling me.

My lawyer's arrival gave me a twinge of hope. They took away the itchy blanket I'd been hugging and made me see James in just the cotton dress and shirt I'd been wearing. Seeing how cold I was, James waved the officers away and gave me his jacket. He followed it up with a cigarette and went into one.

"What the fuck's going on? This is serious! They've got half a kilo to throw at you."

"Me?"

I reeled off the recent events making him listen. Afterwards he asked if I knew someone called Thai; feeling weaker than ever I asked why.

"He was busted big time, some hours ago." Everything made sense and I began to feel delirious. Red had stitched us all up to save his own skin. James put a sandwich in front of me and asked for a hot drink to be brought in.

"Am I getting out of here or what?" I panicked.

"There's more to this bloody mess than just getting out. We're not far away from the new death laws that are about to be enforced!"

I remembered the conversation Kira and I had had with Red about those laws, and I hated him more than ever. I wiped sweat away from my face feeling paranoid. James came towards me and dug into the pocket of the jacket he'd lent me. Putting a hand on my shoulder, he handed me some fags and matches.

"Here, put these away for yourself! I'll do my best to get you into court first thing tomorrow. I can't promise bail, but I'll get the case dealt with before certain deadlines."

He paused and hugged me.

"If it's any consolation, I know you're innocent. The only thing you're guilty of is your addiction, which is something else we've got to work out."

"Right now a hit would be heaven."

"That's exactly what I don't want to hear!"

I tucked the ciggies away as I watched him leave. I no longer knew what to think or which way to turn, and time stood still. Shivering in the cell, I smoked one after the other in a bid to get warm.

I felt my skin cringe as they stood me next to Red in court. I wanted a separate hearing – anything so as not to inhale him. It was weird, really, standing there next to him as if we were complete strangers – as if we'd never so much as shared a cigarette together. As they placed the heroin package in front of the judge, the smell of evil wafted throughout the court and my heart sank. On a verbal level, James put Red to shame, but having previously helped the police he was praised on a very low level. I felt embarrassed for him. He was no more than a twisted worm slithering along his own private gutter.

I pleaded not guilty along with Red, who showed no sign of letting up. After much haggling, bail was granted at five grand apiece. Knowing damn well there was more chance of someone rescuing me rather than him, I smiled.

Back in the court cells, I managed to get a trip to the methadone unit where I drank all my troubles away. By four, there had been no bail paid, just a prison van that was to drop us all at the nearest nicks for the night. Though my vision was blurry from the methadone, I could see Red among the men waiting to be dropped off. I don't think he had actually envisioned reaching the nick where the locals were housed. He must have known he might bump into Thai, because his face began to show signs of regret for the first time. As they called his name, he didn't speak, just joined the queue of inmates leaving the bus.

An hour later, I reached the gates of Tai Tam Gap, a

young offenders' institute high in the mountains.

The officers were cold and dead sticklers for their rules. I entered the remand wing grateful there were only four inmates residing there I sat down in a tacky plastic seat beside the window bars. As I heard keys turn in the lock I began to shiver. A big beefy girl swaggered over to me. She looked like a dyke and spoke only broken English, which suited me just fine, as my social skills were none existent. It was a piss-poor game of verbal charades. Eventually she gave up and retreated back to her part of the room. The screws returned at eight and checked the five of us before we were again locked in together. My clothes were damp from all the hot sweat. Shivering uncontrollably beneath my blanket, I cussed cold turkey and Red alike. I felt a hand on my back. It was the dyke. She had brought me another blanket, which I couldn't refuse. She gave me a nod of acknowledgment before getting her head down with the others.

I drifted in and out of sleep as one does halfway through withdrawal. My mind came to life and did a lot of digesting. I didn't like the hate I could taste, but just the thought of Red increased the pain that was shooting in and out of my head; he had used and abused my good nature, making me feel worthless. I didn't want to think about him or anyone else who had hurt me. Tossing and turning, I drifted off to sleep.

By six in the morning, the screws were back, ensuring that everyone was awake. Depressed, I declined their offer of a shower and breakfast. By ten my bail had been paid and a yellow cab purred outside. Beside it was one of the widest and most welcome smiles I have ever encountered. Combined with freckles it was a face I'll never forget…

Old and New

When someone you know shows up several thousand miles from home, it's weird. When they turn up in a cab outside a jail in the hills, it's freaky. Lolly was a Londoner and had the sweetest of smiles. The sun had darkened her freckles and lightened the tufts of hair poking through her cap.

We'd scrumped apples together, swum in the canals, and eventually enrolled in a typing course that neither of us ever finished. Seeing her was like seeing a ghost, and for a moment, my feet were stuck firmly to the ground. She looked well, but there was no getting away from the tell-tale signs carried by every addict. Hopeful I hurried forward.

"Don't s'pose you got anything on ya?"

She opened the cab door and smiled.

"C'mon, it ain't nice cooking, and the gear's bloody miles away. Why they couldn't build this place downtown like everything else is beyond me."

I glanced down the hill the distance was further than I'd previously taken on board. I felt cold and closed the cab door. I waved the cab onward and made effortless conversation.

"So how come you're here? And how d'ya know about me?"

"Ness … we were having a beer when we heard your name mentioned."

"Is she still in town with all that money?"

"Don't know about any money, but she's in town. Was with a tall guy, is it Jimmie?"

I nodded.

"Everyone wanted to pay the bail, but played pass the butt instead of getting off their own, in the end we did it."

"We…?"

"You remember Zeet, don't ya?"

I pulled an unsure face.

"Anyway, we won some money and decided to give Asia a look. Knew you were somewhere here but Zeet wanted to do India first, so we drew straws and here we are."

Thanks didn't seem enough, so I said nothing and tried to hide the growing disappointment I felt towards the others. By the time we reached town, my jaw ached from all the chat and my bones were rattling bigtime. Staining the sky with its dirty walls and rusty windows, Chung King soon appeared on the horizon. Home to hundreds of travellers and poor Chinese, playground to every dealer and dodgy deal going, it was the biggest dump in the city. I'd scored from it loads, but had always tried to avoid its digs. There was a pile of rubbish blocking some of the entrance which stank. Cats had obviously peed all over it and with the bin men late, the smell was potent.

"God, this place is a shithole!"

I pressed for lift service, while booting a can away.

"It's cheap and cheerful, and the gear's on tap. Rather have the cash than a flash pad like you had."

I raised my eyebrows. "Ness told us all about it, this must be a real comedown."

"Beats kipping with them..." Shuddering I watched the rats rummage through the bags.

"C'mon," Lolly sniggered, "they might climb stairs, but they can't access lifts."

Four flights up and I was another step closer to the gear. As we left the lift, the sound of crying assailed my ears. A few yards farther on, I found a door open. Two hippies, high on heroin, were slumped either end of their bed. Between them, unattended, but safe was a baby. I stood momentarily in the doorway. The room was dirty and made me cringe but something inside me melted. The junkie world was no place for babies – kids or grown-ups for that matter! Their ignorance irritated me. Lolly tugged at me. She stopped three doors down, and opened it. Zeet had just woken up and was in need of a kick-start, knowing gear was only seconds away I let out a huge sigh of relief. Lolly covered the mirror in heroin and handed it to me first. With my nose healed I got fucked up fast, a few moments later Lolly, the crying baby, and Zeet all faded away.

It was the buzzing in my head that woke me some hours later, seeing the room empty I stirred. The swarming sound didn't let up and as I got up the throbbing started. I'd had a similar pain previously in the apartment, but nothing like the one that now materialised. I was busy snorting the pain to death when Lolly entered.

"God, it's busy out there, had to queue for ages to get these."

She shared her satay, and handed me **two** sticks of grilled chicken. It must have been the chewing motion that released the mess in my ears. I felt the gunk trickling before I reached the mirror. Lolly examined my ears and shook her head.

"You need a doctor. You can't just leave that your fucking brain'll get infected!"

"If I had a brain I wouldn't be doing this shit, would I, besides the last doctor I saw cost me dearly."

"I heard!"

"Fuck, is nothing in this city sacred!"

"Seems not…"

Insisting I visit the hospital Lolly didn't let up. Eventually offered to take me, I paused from the snorting, gazed at her genuine concern and put down the note. The building was run down and ridiculous, I'd never seen a hospital quite so horrible. Dirty blankets on broken trolleys made up most of the discarded objects along the hallway. We carried on and saw sheets of cobwebs which hung from the rafters and the smell of urine was a potent reminder of Asian poverty. Fortunate to find a so-called doctor we were directed to a large hall crammed with the city's less fortunate. Plasters, crutches, and bandages decorated the outer benches. Two doctors were using an old table to examine and diagnose from the centre of the room from where they called and dismissed patients at random. A small boy having his leg bandaged was sitting on a chair while his anxious mother watched and waited. It was like a medieval centre for the sick. I wanted to leave, but the pain prevented it. I had no idea who was next, or how their system worked, so, when I was waved over by one of the two doctors, I hesitated. Aware of all the rejected faces homing in on me, I didn't move.

"Hardly fair is it," I turned to Lolly, "these folks probably bin here hours!"

"You of all people should know there ain't no such thing as fair." Lolly forced me up and pushed me forward. "Go on, what you waiting for!"

The doctors were becoming impatient so I approached them and the empty chair.

"Sit. What is problem?"

I pointed to my ears and felt the first doctor poke and prod at them.

"Is a bad infection – drugs?"

"Umm, yeah…"

I watched him tie a thin dressing around a long metal skewer. He pushed it into my ear and continued right down into the side of my neck. I expected it to hurt but strangely enough it didn't. While I tried to switch off from the weird sensation, I watched the other doctor weigh and bag up a whole lot of antibiotics. The doctor repeated the process, dipping his skewer five times before my neck was full. Changing to the other ear he did the same to that one. Movement in my neck restricted, I couldn't hear very well and was beginning to feel dizzy. Feeling like a rag doll I left the hospital like a mobile chemist. Miserable with the pain my spirits were low. Though the mattress at Chung King was rotten it had never seemed more welcome than on my return. Pills mixed with drugs had left me in a zombie state. I sank into it for what could have quite easily have been my last sleep, and entered the dropout zone. Several hours later Lolly woke me and reminded me to sign at the station. She had found some paperwork hanging from my jeans and knew I'd be busted and banged up if I didn't go.

I asked the cab to wait while I went inside the station and tried to sign. Too numb to acknowledge the sneering police, I scribbled on a barely visible line and left them and their ribbing for another night.

After five days of doing the same thing, I felt slightly better. Still unable to hear properly, I couldn't wait to pull out the bandages, the gunk had dried up but the smell was bad. I looked at the mirror and saw that it read, 'Lawyer! Three o'clock'. Lolly had used a pink lipstick to deface it.

I knew I had to go so. While I was searching for soap and shampoo, I saw betting slips all over the place, many of which were big winners, full of wonder I continued with what I was doing.

As I got out of the shower, I could again hear the baby start to cry, knowing that if I didn't hurry my depression would drag me back to bed, I dressed and did one. Two streets down, I saw Fran crossing the road. She had a great glow about her, but never having done heroin probably helped in that department. With bags in both hands, she had been shopping. She clocked me and hurried my way. As she got closer, I saw the bags were full of designer clothes and makeup; putting them down she hugged me.

"I've met someone, Sharm, he's quite wealthy, and well… he's proposed to me!"

"Good for you! And Pang?"

"He's got a whole new crew to work to death!"

As her speech slowed down, she blew a bubble that reminded me of the first time I'd met her.

"Hard to believe it's been a year with all that's gone on," slightly uncomfortable, she undid her top button.

Like everyone else, she knew about Red and the shit he'd showered me with. Since she'd been closest to him, she struggled to talk about it. Like me, she just didn't want to believe any of it. She changed the subject and told me that Jimmie had gone to Japan. His dad had found a whole lot of hash in his bedroom. Furious, he'd sent him to Tokyo to clean up his act and to collect some paperwork for the family business.

"If you're going across town I could share the cab with you." I stopped one and opened the door. "At your service madam..."

Fran got in and accompanied me to my lawyers. The hairdressers made a good stopping point. I had just stepped onto the kerb when Fran called me back. I turned round whereupon she handed me a hundred dollar bill and a piece of her happy gum. Seconds later, the lights changed and she was gone.

James dazzled me with his outgoing personality. He wasn't a miracle worker – just a good guy giving it his best shot. I always knew when a lecture was on its way as he'd tell me one of his awful jokes and fill the kettle. He would then ask me to give up gear for court. That was the bit I always found hard to hear. I didn't see the point, and knew I couldn't cope with the situation clean. He told me that he'd have a court date within days and that with Red still banged up, my chances were looking better than ever. As I returned, my spirits were slightly raised.

With the lift out of order I climbed the stairs. On reaching the third floor I could hear Zeet yelling in excitement. Inside, it was raining cash. Throwing it up and over their heads, Zeet and Lolly raved about a big win they'd had that afternoon. Raining cash, for a moment we all felt rich. Zeet squealed with delight sat down and began to band up the bucks. On a roll, he told me how he'd cleaned up for the second time that afternoon. I'd always known about the track but like many things I'd just never got round to attending. I took the list of evening runners from Lolly sat and studied them. It was exactly what I needed and the prospect of some dosh was even better. As we arrived at the races, the six o'clock was just finishing, and a rolling machine that flattened the grass for the next race charged onto the track.

We approached the bar where we found ourselves bombarded with cheap chat and drink offers. Zeet dismissed them all and ordered three beers, while the waiter busied himself we found a table where we studied the racing programme. Plonking himself down at our table an English gentleman appeared.

"The grey has taken it twice this week. I'm Oscar – Oscar Darlington."

Unable to answer due to a mouthful of peanuts, I raised a hand and smiled.

"Did you say Oscar?" Lolly loved to strip snobs.

"Umm, Darlington. Captain, actually."

"And what are you the captain of?" She asked.

I could see Oscar was irritated by her cheek, but there was amusement too.

"I knew you'd have a sense of humour. So many people lack, it myself included at times."

I stared over the top of my empty glass.

"You live here, Oscar?"

"Intelligent too, what more could one ask for?"

"Another drink..."

Placing his empty on the table, Zeet created an irresistible atmosphere. Oscar was about to get up when a bell rang.

Grooms warming up new runner took to the spruced-up turf and paced. While jockeys prepared themselves the thoroughbreds paraded their beauty and stamina before the grandstands. Leaving the jokes and banter behind we stood up.

"Magnificent creatures..."

Oscar pulled me to the boundary with him. Joined by the others, a debate on winners and losers kicked off. While I chuckled at the clashing energies around me, I absorbed the movement in front. My eyes became fixed on an underweight bay. Smaller than the rest, it appeared weak, but its eyes exhibited passion and power.

"You're not serious?" Oscar sneered at my interest.

"There's determination in its eyes?"

"Non-starter if ever I saw one."

"Aren't you all," I whispered under my breath.

"Well," Zeet scribbled on a piece of paper, "I know where my money's going!" He zipped off.

Decision made I joined him, torn between two runners Lolly and Oscar took a few minutes more before joining us. Buzzing with expectations we placed our bets and sat in silence at the table while starting stalls were filled. As the race began sparks of adrenaline came from almost everyone around us. Momentarily, I remembered what it felt like to be normal, human again and all my woes were drowned, and, for a short while, I was as free as the runners. My horse, though some way to the back, ran well. None of us could hear ourselves think through the cheering and shouting that was rushing round the stadium. As the horses began the last lap my heart began to pound. My horse changed into full throttle, causing unsure speculation and gasps all around.

As the scrawny, underweight bay went into autopilot, the few daredevils who'd bet on him, such as myself, screamed him on to victory. The Chinese and residents were strange folk, liked to go with what they knew not what maybe. Oscar hid his irritation with controlled subtleness, raised his glass and toasted the new Chinese champion, he then and gathered up his newspaper, wallet and pen.

"Well that's me done for today. I'm having some drinks at home there might be a few contacts of interest to you arriving. If you want to join me you can."

Always happy to view new scenery, I was in. Zeet didn't fancy Oscar's invitation of cheesy chat and wine, but Lolly did, so he left us to it.

It took a few minutes to get out of the car park. The gatekeeper was giving away helium balloons, so I tied one to my bag for a laugh. Driving out of the city and into the calmer areas of Honk Kong, the houses looked as if they had been painted upon the hills rather than built. Pretty they were pleasant to see. Arriving at Oscar's many of his guests had already turned up. His maid in attendance she'd had to juggle the bar, kitchen and a variety of conversations a great sigh of relief she smiled at Oscar. Hustling in a large front room various business folks from the city sipped drinks and made the most awful small talk I'd ever heard. A light film of banter upon every smarmy comment was the only thing preventing certain quotes from becoming cat fights or snubbed business deals. Taking a beer I sat down and watched Lolly. Intrigued, she examined pictures, paperwork and some of the framed certificates on various walls. A huge smile on her face, it just kind of grew. Avoiding the small talk I was pleased to see Lolly nod me into the hallway. I followed her into a room where she burst into a fit of giggles.

"D'ya know how much he's worth?"

More interested in one of the two guitars hanging above the first shelf, I shrugged. "Don't know. Don't care."

I took down the guitars and threw one towards her.

"C'mon, let's play."

"This is crazy."

"Good idea."

I untied the balloon and emptied my bag, a Prince tape there I put on. The song was nearly finished when Oscar burst in and began to shout.

"They're antique! Priceless, in fact, and you're playing them!"

While Lolly looked the other way and cried with guilt, I could do nothing but let rip and laugh. It was like being back at school, only Oscar wasn't about to get out a big ruler and belt us with it. Feeling the need to make Oscar smile, I tugged at the balloon and undid the knot, breathing in a bit of the gas I handed it to Lolly. Singing in high pitched tones, Oscar appeared madder than ever.

I gave it up, and let the balloon race around the room till it was empty. Still a bit squeaky, I smiled at him.

"Oh c'mon, Oscar, you gotta see the funny side of it."

His eyes couldn't hide the amusement flooding into them, and he began to simmer.

"C'mon," he said in a lighter tone, "I want you to meet the chief of narcotics he's just arrived and a very good friend of mine." Alarm bells ringing I dreaded the thought. What if he knew about my curfew, recognised me and said something, I didn't fancy any more humiliation.

Oblivious of our bad habits it almost seemed a joke. Feeling uncomfortable we put the guitars back and followed Oscar towards the high hopers mingling in the front room. Seeking out his narcotic friend, Oscar introduced us. The first signs of withdrawal on the horizon I felt slightly cold. Terrified to head for the toilette and snort some of my personal gear, I found myself making small talk to the officer instead. Chatting away to Oscar about various crimes it didn't take long for the subject of drugs to rise. It was quite incredible standing there listening to him describe the downtown drug scenes I knew so well. It was when the warnings began that I decided to head for the loo. Lolly in pursuit we snorted loads.

"I'm actually beginning to enjoy myself," said Lolly.

"Unlike you, I've got to find a way out of here."

"Shit, the signing, I forgot, can't ya nip into town and come back?"

I owed Lolly, finding the maid I asked her to order me a return cab. Nobody saw me leave and nobody but Lolly acknowledged my return. Some hours later the night turned into a sipping, singing, sorry state of affairs, having heard all about stocks and shares, drugs and dealers, good and bad business deals, I retired to one of Oscar's guest rooms where I went out like a light.

By morning, cognac drums were playing in my head and my stomach wouldn't sit still. I could hear the maid so I ventured out to see what was happening. Reading the morning papers, Oscar was being served hot toast.

"Join me," Oscar announced without turning his head.
I hated coffee, but it smelt good, so I drowned myself in decaf. Feeling I had to say something, I blurted out the first thing that entered my head.

"So, Oscar, you used to what, fly, sail or swim?"

"Flew for over twenty years and loved every minute of it. That's how I ended up here. Fell in love with the city and stock market all at once."

"Bet you feel powerful up there, just you and the open sky."

"Sounds good from where I'm standing."

With a towel piled high on her head I can only describe Lolly as a hung-over beehive. Two coffees later, she was buzzing with Oscar's suggestion that we visit Big Wave Bay. Back in the bathroom, we did what heroin was left, hoping the sun would dry me out I was ready.

As we pulled into the cove, we could see waves dancing out at sea. As they got closer to the shore they reared and rolled, gathering height and speed their curls consumed everything beneath them before crashing down on the beach. Oscar took his personalized deck chair and umbrella from the boot. Dragging it across the sand he didn't stop until he found a nice spot to set up. He was too lazy to swim or walk, so we left him watching us with one of his horrible cigars. Stood before the ocean the sight was quite daunting. Pushing and shoving at one another we ended up under the same wave. I had just come up for air when the second was upon me. I swam back with it, and ended up on the shore. We played for hours, teasing each other and running from the waves. It was so good that for a while I forgot I even had a habit. It was exhaustion that eventually forced us out. We rested on the shore and built a big sandcastle. Remembering that Oscar knew the chief of police, I made sure he was sleeping before I crept back and grabbed my bag from beside him. Skinning up we recalled all the cheesy chat and laughed. Turning towards Oscar we tried not to see him as a cartoon figure, quite big he consumed the deck chair, arms spilling over its sides, legs splayed he looked like a giant star fish. Sides hurting from laughter we crawled towards him and took shade under the giant umbrella. Afternoon snooze over, withdrawal creeping in we asked Oscar to take us home. For the first time ever, we felt embarrassed about where we were living, not wanting him to drop us at Chung King, we had him drop us at Seven

Eleven and walked back.

Zeet rolled his eyes. He'd been to the lunchtime races and lost. Pacing the room he blew into the air and spat words at the walls. Eventually, he sat on the bed. "What the fuck am I gonna do?"

Unable to answer, we just smoked. The silence unbearable I was glad to fall asleep.

The next day I saw Zeet leaving a male club, a heroin habit to keep it was pretty obvious what he was selling. Not wanting to cause him any embarrassment I never said a word, not even to Lolly.

Two days of nothing passed, then out of the blue my first case came up, and James got a result. The fine meant I no longer had to sign in at the station every night. The clerk led me down some steps and along a corridor to fill out the final paperwork before I could leave. I entered a busy room where she slapped my case file in front of two officers and left. Twenty minutes later they not only returned my bail money but also my passport. Expecting them to pull another of their sick pranks I took it with hesitation. I knew they were meant to keep it till after the big case, knew it was another of their fuck ups, I breathed deeply, I was free, able to board a plane and leave. I gave it some deeper thought. Maybe they were just waiting to arrest me at the airport. Yeah, that would be more their thing. It was James who snapped me out of it, seeing the passport in my hand he nodded to the law and pointed me towards the exit. Over the moon with their mistake he joined me outside.

"Well, I wouldn't normally say this, but the best thing you can do now is board a plane."

My excitement clouded my thoughts, and, for moment it felt great, then.

"What about the new death sentences? What if they later catch me up and it's all changed?"

His face said it all, they would bring me back to face whatever music was playing at the time.

"I like you Sharm, amongst all the chaos in your head, you're a sensible kid!"

James knew it was right. He just had a big heart. A big hug and I returned to the shithouse.

I had a lot of frustrated steam to get out of my system and Zeet had a lot of gambling debts he'd run up with the Chinese.

"They're gonna kill me!" He yelled over and over.

"Can't you just talk to them, blag a bit more time!" It was lolly.

Zeet pulled a face that said it all.

"Here, I gave him the bail money.

"Right, cheers," he stuttered while shoving it inside his pocket. Liquid intake in mind, me and Lolly went with him. It was a small backstreet bar, inside its occupants were as grimy as the bar itself.

There was no dance floor or friendly faces just tables of tokers who shuffled their feet and cards at the same time. A tall guy got up to meet Zeet. They spoke for ages before they shook hands and agreed on a further game together. Shaking my head me and Lolly sat down and watched.

I'd never been the least bit attracted to the Chinese until I met Lee Lang. At first I took a back seat and waved him off, but his politeness and persistence eventually captured me and I let him get the drinks in. We sat at the bar talking as though we had known each other forever. I made no secret of my habit or situation and by ten we knew quite a bit about one another. He invited me to Hong Kong Island for a dance, and it felt good to be able to go. I jumped down to see what the others were up to and was told they had left. Zeet had lost again, and knew it was better to take it out on the gear rather than the Chinese.

I was impressed to see that Lee had a car. Driving across town, Lee showed me everything from the biggest bank in the world to the ugly, but beautiful, Sharpei dogs which snuffled through the glass of a closed pet shop. On reaching the Island Lee offered to make tea in his apartment, for once the privacy was more appealing than the hectic dance floor I usually loved. Most of the dwellings had been built on steep ridges that caused the car to strain, but three blocks up and we were there.

Lee's upstairs apartment was bare of all but a few cushions, cans, and chopsticks. While Lee made Chinese tea I tinkered with a single hand of backgammon. The tea tasted awful, but I drank it all the same. He pulled out a variety of games that we played and by the early hours I think I'd lost at them all. Yawning I was done for. Lee took my hand and led me into a room.

"Sleep, I have another room."

The steel bed frame had been woven into pretty butterflies. Lee said it was lucky and, since I hadn't had much, I slept well.

I woke early to the sound of running water. With a towel wrapped tightly round him Lee appeared with another cup of green tea. As he put the tea down the dragon tattooed on his belly went all wrinkly and disappeared. Feeling sick from withdrawal I struggled to drink the green tea, not wanting to appear ungrateful, I ventured onto the balcony and poured it into a plant pot there.

Below, people were using the pavements, and the concrete steps, to practice Tai Chi. I watched with great interest as the old wrinklies made all sorts of weird shapes before finally reaching for the sky. Pulling a new shirt over his head Lee joined me.

"How come there are so few foreigners this side?"

"Triads…"

I'd heard about the Chinese mafia and some of their antics. Seeing the uncertainty on my face, Lee elaborated.

"They're not all bad – just making money to survive." He raised his shoulders and curled his mouth to one side. "I do deliveries. Have to help out or I wouldn't make out, it's nothing heavy-like."

It didn't bother me as much as it should have, but then what does when addicted heroin? It has a nasty habit of creeping into your bones and eventually owning you outright. Your thoughts, actions just about everything…

Foreign Cuisine

Zeet's moods became as bad as his debts, so I spent most of my time at Lee's. We got on really well and spent all our time together. I was by now totally into Chinese games, and played around in the bars while Lee did his laundering. With enough of my own shit to worry about, I never asked Lee what he was up to. Sometimes, when he went off for a while, the waiters would give me all sorts of food on the house. Once they gave me a chicken sandwich that tasted a bit sharp. I knew it was something else when they started laughing. On his return, Lee shook a playful fist at them and told me it was snake.

"They're sick."

"They're only playing with you."

"I'd hate to see them pissed off."

"Umm, yeah, you would. Here, try this."

Lee dug into his pocket, and handed me some dry beef to try but the mere smell put me off before it reached my mouth. Back at the apartment he tried to get me to taste everything from chicken claws to herbal sweets. Lee knew that I had to see James at four and insisted on coming. Trying to put the court case to the back of my mind I welcomed the coolness of the connecting underpass. Finding a parking space we walked towards the offices. As soon as we got there, I knew something was wrong. James was sweating and twirling his thumbs repeatedly. Seeing us he slammed the files shut. Forgetting how much I hated coffee, he plugged the percolator in and poured the bad news with it.

"I brought the case forward in order to avoid the new death sentences. What I didn't know was that the bastards were going to change the judge."

At first I didn't answer, I just sat and hoped he had got the wrong client. The door seemed a million miles away. I heard Lee begin to quiz James but my brain had switched off.

"It's a last-minute thing," I heard James say, "very rare to bring a commie in."

I was chain smoking when James slammed down his coffee cup, "Can't you just give it up for court!"

I knew going in to court clean might or might not make a difference, but putting it into practice at this stage seemed more impossible than ever before. Heroin had me by the neck and soul, its hold strong there was nothing I could do about it.

I went downstairs and counted cars. I couldn't help but wish I'd mixed with the Chinese sooner. All I'd done was encounter foreign faces from the start. After all, I mean, wasn't that why I'd left, to escape bullies, British bullshit and hypocrisy. I was being hard on myself for trusting Red. Unlike him, at least I had a soul, even if it was temporarily numb.

Knowing there was little to say, Lee suggested we leave the car and take the ferry back. He said the sea would do me good. He was right the cooling mist moistened my skin and helped me relax. The walk up the steep hills left us tired and parched. We took clumps of ice from the fridge, smashed them up, and doused them in lemonade. Watching the bubbles swirl around in the ice reminded me of the many addicts in the city. While I took a shower, Lee took a telephone call. Getting a lift to Kowloon he collected his car. Returning he asked me if I wanted to visit an Island with him.

We drove to the other end of town and boarded a small boat. Peng-Chau was a dark and gloomy little island some twenty minutes from the mainland. I could feel the island's stagnant energy before we arrived. It was such a small place, there were no cabs, and, to my surprise, the streets were bare, but as we walked down the first, oldies began to poke their heads through dirty windows. I think they had all forgotten how to smile – either that or they were frightened.

As we turned into the last street, the smell of death hit us. A few yards on, maggots crawled from the carcass of a rotting dog, as they moved about so the smell spread. Five minutes later we were knocking on an old door. Our first knock was ignored. We were about to give the door a boot when it opened. Giving us a nod to enter, a frail figure closed the door behind us. In the middle of the room, triads were counting money on an old table top, one of them leant back and called out. A moment later infection filled the room and our lungs alike. I coughed, stepped back and cupped my mouth in order to avoid the foul air the third party carried in with him. A fire in his chest it was roaring with infection.

The conversation quickly become harsh, I think they were moaning at Lee for either being late or bringing me. The tallest of the gang kept pointing and shouting my way. I didn't see what the big deal was – it wasn't like I even spoke the language. Lee stood his ground and shouted back. The word 'dulay' was repeated the most. Lee threw a package on the table and folded his arms. The vultures disappeared out back and returned with a parcel of used notes. Lee winked at me, opened the door and we left.

"It's all a big front. They like to think they're bigger than they are, but they ain't, courtesy of this."

He shoved his hand inside my jeans pocket, accidentally pinching me as he did so. Pulling out my personal stash of heroin, he waved it in the air.

"It's no good, you know."

Ignoring the comment I retrieved the gear from him. "And the row…?"

"Over you... I told 'em you were cool but being the first foreigner 'ere, they're being paranoid."

"Black market business island aye!"

"Could say that…!"

I cast my mind back to Harry and the posh yacht party. I somehow couldn't imagine him, or Claudia, anywhere near the place doing dodgy deals with triads. The thought of

Claudia clomping about gave me something to take my mind off the event. The boat owner seemed as pleased as us to be leaving, I watched as he steered through the water pleased to see the distance between us and the dock disappear. It looked like hard work, but he seemed to be at one with the technique he'd mastered over a lifetime.

While I counted clouds, Lee counted his money. Leaning on me, Lee asked if I wanted to visit his family with him. At first, I didn't know what to say, but after a few minutes I decided it would be nice. We left the boat and got a cab up the side of Tong Gung – another part of town I'd never seen. The sloping streets eventually became too steep to drive up, so we left the car and walked the last few laps. As we reached one of the oldest tower blocks, we embarked upon our final climb, the stairs.

The small balconies were cracked and covered in bird mess. Glancing down, I realized we were near the top and felt a terrible wave of vertigo come over me. Lee grabbed me and led me several doors down to where his mother met us with open arms. His father entered, wanting to know what all the commotion was about. I hadn't a clue what they were on about, only that I felt comfortable with them. It was easy to see how Lee had got to be what he was – the way his family lived was no way of living. The flooring was made up of small rugs that covered heat cracks, and what little furniture there was, was so old I don't think even flames would want to engulf it. His mother told us to make ourselves comfortable and insisted on cooking for us.

Lee's father was thin and frail. He'd worked all his life in one of the local factories, where he had earned just enough for food and the rent they paid each month, but it had taken its toll. When he could no longer carry the heavy pallets, they had tossed him aside and replaced him with someone who could. Wanting to change the subject, I noticed a small shrine on the cabinet that caught my attention; beautifully kept with fresh flowers, incense, and a small photo. I approached it for a closer look.

"It's Mumma." His father looked proud for the first time.

Returning from the back streets, Lee's younger brother brought a commotion home with him. Waving a handful of cards in the air, still arguing with his opponent, he burst into the lounge.

"He's still learning to cheat," Lee grinned.

He slapped his brother's head and put the hand right. His dad put his finger to his mouth and followed the gesture with a long "shhhhhhh." I could only presume he didn't want Lee's mother, who was still in the kitchen, to be upset. Several minutes later she appeared with small flower-covered bowls, which she placed on the table, after which she handed out chopsticks. I practised using them, but struggled to capture as much as one grain of rice.

I caught snippets of their conversation and knew they were discussing my case. Every so often I would hear the word Inglessee followed by big smiles that washed all the shit away. They ate so quickly I was surprised they had any time to talk at all. With three empty bowls on the table, I took a Chinese spoon and finished mine. After our meal, Lee sat and counted the money he had collected from the island before handing it to his father. To see the old man's eyes find some further meaning other than despair was nice. As we headed back we saw Lee's brother playing on the stairs, we stopped, dug deep into our pockets and gave him all our change. The little lad took the cash, jumped into the air and made off.

"Can't you get them a place? Any where's gotta be better than here."

"My place ain't secure, what happens to 'em if I ain't around? Nah, they can't take any more heartache, better what they know than the streets."

James had often said to pop in if I happened to be passing, you never know, there might be news. That was the day I wished I'd we'd just kept going, been unable to get parked, stayed at the apartment with his folks, anything but hear the news James had to bear. It was the day what should have been good news became bad. Red was out. Someone had paid his bail, and he'd done a bunk. It was my worst nightmare yet! I was up shit creek and I knew there were no paddles without Red. Lee cussed Red in Cantonese, saying he would send half the city out to find him but I knew it was too late for all that. Red might not have been born in the city, but there were enough dives for him to slither into, and he knew them all. The telephone rang, James sounded miserable, asking why, what, who and when over and over again. His eyes kept flitting around and the pen he kept tapping on the table turned into a pneumatic drill. The sudden surge of compassion in his eyes indicated something seriously wrong. He put down the telephone and gazed up.

"Tomorrow," he said in a soft tone, "In order to avoid possible death penalties the case is tomorrow!"

Dizzy from too much information I got up and left. Chung King was close, so while Lee informed some of the locals, I climbed the stairs to Lolly's. She sat, smiling, on the end of her bed, fiddling with a new Walkman. On seeing my face, she got up and gave me a hug. Sitting down she listened to everything.

"D'ya know why they invented thrush?" A bit bewildered I stared at her. "So we could get used to irritating cunts!"

My emotions were riding high and came out in waves of laughter. Cracking joke after joke all Lolly could do was make me laugh. Sometime later, I saw Lee stood in the doorway, arms folded he frowned.

"Don't worry, it's perfectly normal." Creeping up behind Lee it was Zeet.

"Come on," Lee said, "I got a surprise for you." Lee held out a hand and hauled me up. "You's also if you want to join us?" He looked at the others.

Lolly grabbed her bag and Zeet his gear. Rolling across town, *'Take My Breath Away'* was playing on the radio. As I listened to it, the city and its lights began to vanish. Turning left, engine straining we headed up towards a dirt track. We took it as far as the car was capable, parking up we all got out and began walking, climbing up and around the edge, there didn't seem to be much other than steep rock face but, insisting it was worth the walk and wait, we followed Lee. I hoisted myself over a harsh piece of rock and my breath really was taken away. I think it was the same for all of us. The view was monumental. Sprinkled with glitter and star gifts the sky was an eternal sheet of silk that shimmered and shone. Framing the universe a royal blue streaked around and about the stars. The city seemed a million miles away, dazzling and dancing just as it had done that very first night I'd arrived, only now the innocence had been lost forever.

"It's amazing."

Standing behind to me, Lee put his hands on my shoulders.

"I wanted to show you something unforgettable. Dad brought me here when I little, and he was able. Pretty, huh? Come, there's a boulder over there, let's sit and make a smoke."

Unable to take my eyes away from the sky I grabbed his hand and followed my feet.

Speechless, Zeet and Lolly followed. Sitting on his heels Zeet also skinned-up. It was a beautiful but strange time for me, insecurities creeping in and out like the oxygen I was breathing. I felt the bad buzz creep in and buckled.

"You will all visit, won't you?"

Lee shook his head and swallowed hard, turning to the

others, I collected half-smiles and head-shakes. I don't know what I expected them to say, they could have made something up, anything to make me feel better, anything but the cruel silence all around us. But had they lied I wouldn't have liked that either. We sat up there for some hours, smoking joint after joint, counting star after star. I wondered how Kira was doing, what it would have been like had I been able to go with her. I glared up, 'life's what you make it I heard my father saying. Well, I've certainly fucked mine, I thought. It wasn't easy getting my arse off the rock. Glued to it, I tried not to guess what the morning held.

"C'mon," said Lee, "we can all crash at mine, go together in the morning!"

Returning to Lee's apartment none of us slept, we just played hand after hand of cards. For weeks I had pretended it was all a joke – some sort of silly dream – a mistake. But by eight I knew it wasn't. I glanced at Lee. He was resting his eyes and, as long as they were closed the situation was easier to harbour, pretend it was all a bad joke, even waking up with the rats seemed a better solution.

My hands trembled so much I couldn't even crush a line without soaking it in sweat. Lolly took over, emptied the whole bag out and began to crush up. Before leaving, I had cleared most of the mirror and felt pretty numb. We knew that James would be expecting his money, so we all dug deep, but it was nowhere near enough. Only hundreds instead of thousands, I really expected to have to go it alone. In the court lobby, waiting with his leather briefcase and matching shoes, James shuffled uneasily. Approaching him I began discussing his finances. He raised a hand and called me into a room where he explained that financially things had all been taken care of.

"How…?" I stuttered.

"Kira, your friend Kira settled the debt via cheque yesterday."

"Why didn't you tell me?"

"Because if you remember you left before I had a chance to. I also received a cheque with a Valentine, signature on it."

"Good old Harry, news travels fast aye!"

"I used it to ease things in the court, I'll explain later."

At that moment my name was called and the conversation ceased. Judge Pang didn't speak a word of English and was every bit the misery he looked. While the case was read out he made no secret of his boredom, rolling his eyes before the clerk he twiddled his pen and tapped it along the bench top before him.

While they played ping pong with my life, Lee frowned. Catching my eye, he projected what positivity he could before eventually bowing his head. While Lolly looked down I saw Zeet leave the court. Voices raised and paperwork slammed the court became silent. Led away by two officers I knew it was bad news. In the cells downstairs, I knew nothing till James arrived.

"Two weeks remand," he puffed, "its, good…"

"What's good about it?"

"You'll soon be clean."

My heart sank as I sat down. Handing him some cash I asked him for some cigarettes. While he was gone a young Thai girl entered. Tearful she sat twiddling her hands, sniffing every few minutes. James returned with the cigarettes and a bar of chocolate which I gave to the girl. An hour later I was driven towards Changmai and detained in a women's jail. As the gear wore off so the reality of things hit me. By the time I reached the assessment office my legs were blubber and my bones were being hosed out with icy water. The closest I was going to get to any kind of pain relief was by being in the hospital but not before going through all their humiliating bullshit first. A strip search was absolute hell, the internal one even worse. I asked when we would get some methadone. The sarcastic smirks were answer enough. It really pissed me off that the drug capital of the world failed to supply a proper drug detox system, so it was DIY or die in public. There was no methadone, just the odd aspirin that the screws seemed to enjoy offering out. I was perspiring and running out of patience, and was glad I didn't speak Cantonese. After the final torture of showering, I felt like a fully-set sick jelly. With everyone recovering from different stages of cold turkey the hospital wing was quiet. I wobbled towards an empty bed where I passed out. The sound of banging and buckets stirred me. Taking their bowls, women with distorted features queued for breakfast. Rice bowls filled the screws then dished up the entrails. I was hungry but in the first deep stage of definite pain, I was too weak to move, and, since no one was going to fetch me any rice, starvation seemed a simple option till the lunchtime shift.

As my legs gradually regained a certain amount of strength, I managed to join the queue for food and venture to the loos. After a week, they told me I was well enough to participate in proper prison life. A hall full of Chinese and I was in main circulation. This I found hardest of all, still suffering from headaches and shakes I struggled to answer the inquisitive inmates who wouldn't leave me alone. A singer from Shanghai, who was fluent in English, rescued me. She gave me a well-needed cigarette but the screws refused to light us up. I burst into tears and just wanted to die. There was nothing to do, not even for the long-term prisoners who constantly asked for work and crafts to pass the time. It was a small institute that failed to supply anything other than time and space.

Two weeks later, it was time to go back and receive the final sentence. Petrified of facing the world stone cold sober, I pretended I was just boarding a bus across town. I counted cars, high- rise buildings and read advertisements. I even redesigned some of them in my mind. I searched for animals along the way. I hadn't seen many since my arrival, surely there had to be some wildlife? Finally, I acknowledged my emotions and wondered what Lee and the others were doing, where Kira was, but most of all, where that bastard Red was.

Lost Liberty...

I was pleased to see James, but he didn't stop for long, just threw me some fags and made off up the steps in a new suit and short back and sides. I counted each step till he reached the top. Taking them in twos as I went up to court, I beat his time. Stupid I know but when you're in a spot like that the mind tends to use anything as a diversion.

In the court they were all there, the judge and hangman, the onlookers and supporters. Just as Lee wore his best suit, so Lolly did her famous smile. The court was a whirlwind of conversational confusion. I watched James argue my case in Cantonese, but it didn't take long for PC Pang to dish out his orders and give me a worthless wave away. Downstairs, James told me he'd got the sentence reduced from three years to one.

"Take it that's where Valetine's money went?"

He nodded a yes. At first it was all too much and I just cried. He opened a new pack of Rothmans, sat me down and told me that I'd go back to Tai Tam Gap, the young offenders set high in the mountains.

"Look on the bright side. We missed the life thing, and you've got all yours in front of you." He clenched his fists, "and, if Red turns up, we'll nail the bastard," he paused. "You know Thai got five years, don't you? Imagine how he feels."

After the shock had sunk in we sat and chatted for ages. It was weird, really. We could have been anywhere, anywhere other than jail. He squeezed my hand and promised me a supply of books when he had a minute. I knew he would probably be too busy to bother. But that was cool he had done enough. I watched him leave with a heavy heart, deep down I knew I'd never see him again.

The only one destined for the Gap, I didn't have to wait long for a lift. Driving back up the long tracks I was allowed one last smoke. From the back window I inhaled deeply watching the city disappear into a tiny dot as I did so. I was okay until we arrived. That's when the confusion and insecurity crept into my bones, alongside the chills of withdrawal I began to buckle. That's when I felt like an alien just arriving on another planet for inspection.

As the gates opened and the language barriers kicked in, my heart began to thump, and, for a moment, I thought it was going to leave my chest. Young inmates with crew-cut hair darted about the place, desperate to impress and avoid confrontation of any sort with the screws. Nervous and afraid of what the future held, I just kept one foot moving in front of the other. The desire for drugs became overwhelming, an urge that would send me insane if I didn't get a grip. As they took my watch, chain, and freedom, visions of Red tanning himself in the sun taunted my mind. Marched downstairs into an office I was given the third degree and told if I didn't behave they would begin by shaving my hair like some of the others I had seen. Exchanging my jeans and t shirt for a thin cotton dress I tied back my hair and begrudgingly put on the boots they pushed my way.

"Will I get anything for withdrawal…?" The look on their faces was answer enough. "How about a cigarette…?"

The officer in change slammed down her pen. "In case you haven't noticed you're in the young offender's institute. If you want cigarettes, then you can go back to the women's prison down town!"

I sensed a hard ride ahead. Bones still jittering and skin still crawling I tried to stand still. Once the paperwork was done, I was led into a concrete exercise area where I had to wait before being piled up with blankets and shoe polish. I was then taken down some steps towards a grey building dressed in black bars. With itchy blankets piled high in my arms, I stood in the doorway. To my left Thais and Vietnamese girls occupied one of the tables. The Chinese, who were pretty hostile, occupied the others, when they weren't dishing out dirty looks they whispered relentlessly. I heard my name being scratched on a blackboard, a few harsh words relayed in Cantonese and I was left alone. Weak, withdrawn, and totally strung out, I wanted to die, or wanted someone to slap my face really hard and wake me up. I heard the gate being locked. A glance over my shoulder and the screws had gone. Engulfed in foreign eyes I felt really uncomfortable. There were four sleeping areas turning to my left, I saw my name and a row of fibre glass beds. Entering I sat on one. There was no heating, and the cold began to gnaw away at me like a hungry animal. I curled up on the bed hugging the blankets I rubbed my hands hard, if I could just get the blood flowing I thought. Hearing voices I sat up to see several Thai girls stood around me...

"I'm Wancham." The first of them said.

Her English was good. She sat next to me and told me the beds were out of bounds during work hours. She also explained about remand, remission, all the boring stuff that only mattered to inmates. Relieving me of my blankets she put them on the end of the bed.

"Come, if you stay in here they will send you downstairs. It's even colder there."

"What, we just gotta sit in that hall?"

"It's better than below," her face changed, "believe me." Pulling my arm, she convinced me to get up and join the prisoners. The Chinese despised me for creating conversation with the Thais. They hissed and grumbled over everything and nothing till I despised them back for being so pathetic. Returning to the entrance, I gazed through the bars onto the concrete which surrounded us. A chill saturated me and the air turned to ice. Rain came, growing steadily heavier like my heart. Gathering speed it fell like sheets of transparent paper pushing itself as well as the dirt and gravel over and down the mountain. Goosebumps emerged all over me and the flimsy dress I was wearing did nothing to combat my low body temperatures. I kept telling myself that someone would visit, that someone would bring me a bit of powder, anything to stop my mind from whirling with emotions. The drug world was anything but easy to understand and withdrawal the biggest bastard on the planet. Out of sight, I was certainly out of everyone's mind. The fact that Red could end all my torture was too much. I broke. I cried, craved for a fag, would have done anything for a drink, and would have given my life for wings.

Eventually I prayed for strength. Seeing me upset, Wancham, the young Thai girl, placed a hand on my shoulder, I felt warmth and genuine concern, after that, I got on with it.

I welcomed lockup, but the sleep I longed for just didn't arrive. The drugs still vacating my system, my mind was now alive and kicking. No longer numb, feelings raw, I was really struggling. Being the only English girl there, my cellmates wanted to know everything. Then I had to listen to all their stories, after which they all finally got some sleep. Sleepless, I churned into a pit of semi consciousness. It was the banging on the bars that bought me out of my hazy consciousness. I saw the girls leap to their feet and stand to attention.

"Up..!" Wancham waved her arms at me.

Obliging, I got on my feet. The shouting stung my ears, a minute later Madame, head of the prison entered and examined us and our beds. A click of her fingers and blankets were folded and girls dressed. Once done we stood to attention until told otherwise. One last nod and we were allowed to enter the hall. Bowls dished out and we cued for breakfast. While young prisoners from the other side of the building dished the rice up, the screws dished the meat up. Bypassing the gristle it was rice only for me. Its warmth gave me enough energy to get by. Outside, it was line-up and boot inspection. It was amusing to see the reaction of Madame as she walked down the line up subjecting some to a clout and others a nod. Dull, my boots got me a grilling. It was soon apparent that dull boots led to verbal abuse and humiliation. After inspection, we were split into two and sent to either the laundry or the class room. Mush Tang, the head of laundry, like so many others, hated the foreigners. He didn't give orders he just stared until his message was transmitted through tiny evil eyes. A box of rags and he pointed me towards it. Once the others were all working, a glint of happiness in those piggy eyes he took one of the rags and folded it in four, grunting he then tossed it aside and left me to it. It was a twisted act of mind torture. Folding rags on the floor was the pits, but out back, as I discovered, was also the warmest place to be, inside the prison. Three hours later, we were queuing for lunch. The congie (water left over from cooked rice) was like grey sludge and something that most of us passed on. Hungry, we all spent the hour fiddling back in the dorm. After that I found myself in the classroom above the main gates. Of course, for me it was mental torture because I didn't know Cantonese, and no one gave a shit, so the time dragged like mad.

We shared showers after which we received supper, followed by what I quickly named the 'dead time'. a time everyone spent shining her boots with the polish provided. Wondering how I was going to manage, I didn't sleep, secretly I was falling apart.

The following morning Mush Tang began shouting at one of the Thais. In fact he made her so nervous that she forgot her hand was inside the steamer and shut the giant metal lip down on it. Her screams brought the laundry to a standstill. As they lifted the machinery, her skin came away and she was rushed to the infirmary. Mush Tang had a hard time concealing the guilt that crept into his face. The smell stayed long after they took her away. I didn't want to clean the machine, and was grateful he didn't ask me to. Ordering us all back to work, his temper was worse than usual, and lunch couldn't come soon enough. While we waited to go to class, the prison nurse brought the Thai girl back. They had given her nothing for the pain, just an old cloth to hold over the scald. Still in agony, she cried heavily. I tried to comfort her, but doubt she understood anything I was actually saying. Ming Jute, one of the long-term Chinese prisoners, joined me. She inspected the injury and spoke to her fellow inmates who rummaged through their lockers for tubes of toothpaste. Assuring the girl it would relieve her pain, they squeezed the stuff repeatedly covering the injury.

Still trying to stop her tears, the girls tried to make her

laugh. It took over a week for the skin to heal slightly but heal it did. Once a month, everybody received a wage. My allowance was one of the smallest due to the unimportance of the job I'd been given. Watching the Chinese exchange their allowance for face creams was like torture, as my skin felt like sandpaper. Since I knew that I had nowhere near enough money for such luxuries, I watched in envy as they soaked themselves in hard-earned softness. Sick of my monotonous existence, I decided that if they weren't going to speak to me I'd damn well learn their lingo and speak to them. And so the classroom became my inspiration. Only God knew how much I needed some. I liked learning, and when the sun shone it was the brightest room to be in. Learning the language became a fulltime occupation and so I started reading, writing, and pronouncing Cantonese. The harder the symbols, the more determined I was to conquer them. My determination also brought me respect from the officers. It was just small things to begin with – like warm smiles instead of the cold shoulder they were so good at giving. The more I spoke their lingo, the friendlier they became, and so the wall eventually came down. Seeing this, Ming Jute really warmed up to me, and every evening we exchanged languages. While I helped her with her English, she helped me to expand my Cantonese eventually she even shared her face cream with me.

There was nothing good about prison but as the barriers came down so life became slightly easier. The turnover of foreign faces was rapid. Most Asians made their way to Hong Kong to sell their souls for a fast buck in order to return home and provide food for their families. However, the penalty for getting caught was three months in jail followed by a fast deportation back home. As I wondered what they would do with me, many thoughts began to flow. A few days later, I was called into the office and was one step closer to finding out my fate. They told me that Red had been found and was due in court, which brought on mixed emotions. My attendance was required, and there was a possibility that I would be set free if he was found guilty. I was bursting with excitement as I returned to the dorm but seeing Ming Jute, my few months suddenly seemed insignificant and I cooled it. She was serving eight years for a haul of shit that her boyfriend had bestowed upon her; knowing she didn't deserve one second of it, I shut up. But she had been around long enough to know that you didn't get called up for nothing and insisted I tell her. Knowing I felt bad because of her, she smiled.

"It's okay. You go get out, men, they all weak."

"Weak, they're fucking wankers!"

"What is wankers...?" She asked.

Interpreting this little meaning by hand to the whole nick, the following hour became a bundle of laughs.

Two days later, I was driven into town and taken back into the courts. Inside the holding cell I suddenly heard a familiar voice. Hearing him caused a tidal wave of resentment to run through my body. I didn't answer, just listened to him plead and beg. There was nothing he wasn't going to get me if I didn't enter the court and if I finished my sentence without a fuss. I knew that he was chipping away at the soft spot he'd used so often in the past and I tried to ignore him. I heard his door being unlocked, he paused before me. I barely recognized him beneath the weight he'd gained, his neck was at one with his shoulders, and the short hair the nick had given him made his round face look like a puff adder shedding a hangover. Twenty minutes later, he was free. Deliberately smiling, he asked the officer for a smoke and lit it in front of me, it was in that moment I realized that I'd never known him at all, that the brown stuff had corroded and corrupted his mind beyond repair. Or perhaps he'd simply been born the bastard he really was. Either way his behaviour was a fucking disgrace. Instead of being angry I was just glad to be me and not him. He puffed several times before finally leaving, that was the last I ever saw of him.

Having observed everything, my officer took me into a back room and told me that because the case had already been done and dusted, the courts couldn't be bothered to dig it all up again. It was easier to just accept his not guilty plea and keep me, way of the world she said. She also said that the courts had issued me with a deportation order. Seeing my disappointment, she left the cuffs off and offered me a fag. Half way up the mountain she gave me another and another. It was during the last part of the journey that I did a lot of thinking. I had five months left, and I damn well wasn't going spend it on the floor folding dust rags. I knew Mush Tang either gave in to prison whims or made people pay for asking. He liked to send souls back to the land of non-existence, and I knew that if I asked for anything I would be taking a gamble, especially since I was a mere foreigner. The next morning I marched right up to Mush Tang and asked to be promoted beside the top Chinese who did the ironing. A hint of amusement in those piggy eyes he found the request more of a challenge.

"Come." He demoted a Cambodian, but doubled the ordinary workload. "If it's done you keep the post."

With Ming Jute's help, I ironed the shirts and trousers and had them ready by lunchtime for the factory that took advantage of our free services.

Last Lights
Take My Breath Away

Nothing interesting ever happened in the Gap, so, when one of the younger inmates from downstairs jumped the wall, it created a lot of excitement. She gave good chase down the mountain weaving through the trees and waving two fingers behind her, but they headed her off and caught up at the bottom. Having learned a lot of the language, I could understand the cussing as she was taken to solitary. The rest of the day was filled with normal routine that quickly passed into evening again. Now I was able to talk to and understand the other girls, conversations were a pleasure rather than a chore and when it came to lockup Wancham would tell me all about Thailand and its delights, she also taught me much of her language. The day she was released, I knew I was losing a good companion and the best chatterbox in the joint. She had helped me get through many a depressing night with her hilarious and controversial stories.

My mind had long buried thoughts of Lee or anyone else that I might have expected to visit, so when the screws told me that Zeet was in the waiting room, it's safe to say I was shocked. I had put thoughts of heroin on hold, but, as I neared the room, they came flooding back like a tidal wave. I had no idea what he wanted, and couldn't wait to find out what everyone was up to. Unable to speak he got up and gave me a heartfelt hug; but for the screws I think he would have hugged me forever.

"I'm going to India," he said eventually, "going for good."

I didn't answer but just listened. He told me that Lee had got into bother just days after my hearing. A dodgy deal in the New Territories had got out of hand and he'd gone to jail for six months. I knew something major was up by the way he kept fiddling and shuffling about. It was in the atmosphere and all around us. His voice became quiet and his eyes began to moisten. Stuttering, he told me Lolly was dead. She'd intravenously got sloshed downtown on cocaine till she choked in a pool of vomit. His voice trailed off into an echo, but somewhere among those mumbled words, I heard him saying that, had they known Red was gonna be there, they wouldn't, because he was the one dishing out the gear.

After that I didn't hear anything else he had to say, I just kept getting flashbacks and visions of Lolly, outside the gates. Like the stars, her smile was bright and unforgettable. I had a dazzling image of her that I would always keep in my mind. Back in the dorm I spent the rest of the day trying to shake off what he'd said. Angry, I cussed Red, even cussed Zeet at one point for the visit. Why hadn't he just stayed away! Why did he have to come now? My frustration grew in fact it landed me in a whole lot of shit with a Thai bird. The row was over nothing, but nothing can be everything in prison. She'd brushed past me and, without thinking I told her to fuck off in her own language. She swung out at me. I hit her back and the screws ended it. There were only two holding cells, and one was already occupied, so I was spared the unpleasantness of it. When I heard that the girl was up for release, I felt guilty at having cost her a few extra days. I had to face the fact that heroin had ruined everything and was going to haunt me forever. From then on there wasn't much that registered, right up to the night before my own release. I was frightened of what was ahead of me and spent all my time tracking the glow bugs through the dorms and out into the dark. There, they splashed the night with raw energy that followed them like fireworks. Unlike most people they knew what they were doing, where they were going and how to get there. My mind a maze of past and present events I didn't sleep well.

The morning was filled with warm farewells. A string of kisses, hugs, and handmade cards devoured me from every angle. The girls had stolen stuff from the classroom, risking more than they should have. A part of me had grown to love their natural, disciplined ways. I had grown accustomed to their food and the simplicity of their lives. As the guards arrived I turned a key in my heart. Goodbyes are never easy, so I didn't look back.

Visions of Lolly in my head, I dreaded the final gate where she'd once been. As we arrived, it was a weird almost unreal moment. As the gates opened, so my tears flowed.

I spent three days at passport control, where I tried to make sense of everything, but there is no sense in drugs. My mouth tasted bad, and my memories of Asia would always be bittersweet. When the people you trust let you down, it scars. When the people you care about die, it leaves a hole in your soul.

The flight was long and drawn out. I thought about home, the one place I'd always held true to my heart, but knew my dad would be unsupportive and unsympathetic. I wanted to feel numb again, and fought my feelings all the way back. It was a force I cannot describe, a power strong enough to pull us all over the edge.

Drugs will make you feel mighty
but weightless within minutes.